A Handbook
For
Higher Education And Campus
Ministry
In The
Annual Conference

by
Robert H. Conn, Director
Annual Conference Relations and Public Policy Programs
Division of Higher Education
General Board of Higher Education and Ministry

A publication of the Division of Higher Education of the General Board of Higher Education and Ministry, P. O. Box 871, Nashville, Tennessee 37202.

ISBN 0-938162-10-1

Contents

Introduction

This *Handbook* more than refurbishes the recent *Manual for the Annual Conference Board of Higher Education and Campus Ministry*. It replaces it. The 1988 General Conference of The United Methodist Church made significant changes in section 732 of the *Book of Discipline*. Those changes clarified many areas of the work of the Annual Conference Board of Higher Education and Campus Ministry. This *Handbook* registers those clarifications.

The General Conference also tightened many of the lines between the Annual Conference Board and other agencies of the annual conference. For example, it is clear now that the Board manages the conference's relationship to conference-related schools and colleges and that it sets policies for the election of Wesley Foundation Boards of Directors.

The General Conference also expanded the involvements of the Board. The Board now becomes a key player in the selection of Wesley Foundation Directors and has increased membership on Area Commissions.

Those changes and others required a fresh guidebook. But what required those changes? They eventuated from a set of consultations that occurred in the middle of the 1984-88 quadrennium. At that time, the Division of Higher Education of the General Board of Higher Education and Ministry sponsored hearings in each jurisdiction. Selected Annual Conference Board chairs and General Board representatives convened to review the then current *Book of Discipline* section on the Annual Conference Board of Higher Education and Campus Ministry. They focused on ways the *Discipline* could enable the Annual Conference Board to do its work.

Those consultations resulted in a preliminary set of proposals for improving the legislation affecting the Annual Conference Board. Those proposals then went to constituents of the Boards—college presidents and campus ministers. Then they were published in the newsletter for Annual Conference Boards: *New Perspectives*. The newsletter invited response.

The final legislative proposal was then drawn up, reviewed by the elected membership of the General Board of Higher Education and Ministry, and sent on to General Conference, where it passed without dissenting vote. It was the first time that legislation for the Annual Conference Board had been built from the ground up by the very people who had to carry out that legislation. The value of their contribution can be measured by the pertinence of their proposals.

The extent of some of the changes is quite large. Further, their implications are not always obvious at first. Nor are techniques for enacting the legislation locally. For those reasons this *Handbook* has assumed a somewhat different character from the previous *Manual.* It is longer, in a different order, and has many more pages on programs. But its cardinal difference is that it includes detailed commentary on each of the new or altered paragraphs in section 732 of the 1988 *Book of Discipline.* That commentary performs two tasks: it interprets the legislation, and it suggests ways of carrying it out. Major sections of the chapters on schools, colleges, and universities and campus ministry—and to a lesser extent of the chapter on public policy—contain that commentary. They also include several program ideas as well as sections on special issues in each area.

Other chapters deal with organizing the Board. Two of them—one on planning and one on organization and membership—are simplified but otherwise similar to the older *Manual.* Those have been placed later in the *Handbook* than in the *Manual.* It seemed best to discuss program first, deferring questions about organization until after that. Form follows function. The chapter on Area Commissions pulls the information from the *Manual* in line with the new legislation.

The chapter dealing with programs of the general church is larger, and offers some ideas about the new Africa University. It needed also to adjust to changes in the general church's emphasis on ethnic minority ministries.

A short chapter has been added at the beginning, noting the benchmarks in United Methodist ministry in higher education. Its strategy is simply to denote the events that have created the current circumstances we all have to deal with in church-related higher education. It arises from that hope that an ounce of history will be worth more than a pound of perturbation.

Many people have helped to make the *Handbook* possible. The many Annual Conference Board chairs who consulted or responded to inquiries, the college presidents and campus ministers who offered advice, and the elected members of the Division of Higher Education all will see their imprints here. The staff of the Division of Higher Education has provided a sustaining pool of expertise: Ken Yamada, Allan Burry, Shirley Lewis, Helen Neinast, and Richard Hicks. Melanie Skeeters has gone through repeated editings with secretarial patience and skill. To them I express gratitude, and along with them express the hope that this will prove a useful tool for ministry in higher education.

Robert H. Conn

Nashville, Tennessee

June, 1989

Chapter One

Ministry In Higher Education

United Methodist ministry in higher education is as old as Methodism itself. When the Methodists formed their denomination at the Christmas Conference in 1784 they did two things that set their stamp upon their style of Christianity: they elected General Superintendents (bishops) and they founded Cokesbury College. Episcopacy and education have been with Methodists ever since.

By the end of their first half century, Methodists had started schools and colleges all along the eastern seaboard. At the half century point they picked up the pace. Before they had finished, they had founded or associated with more than a thousand schools, colleges, and universities and created an educational enterprise that spread from the Atlantic, over the sprawling western frontier, to the shores of the Pacific.

While the United Methodists and their predecessor denominations had specific hesitations about aspects of education, they never stopped the enterprise. Some debated about whether the church should educate clergy ("preachers should be God-made not man-made"). Others worried early over support. Racial prejudice flawed some approaches. Even in the heat of debate, however, Methodists chartered new campuses and laid the bricks for new buildings.

By the late nineteenth century, General Conference asked each annual conference to establish a college within its precincts. Many conferences already had more than that. Several had systems of feeder elementary schools as well.

Clearly education, and particularly higher education, had great vitality in the Methodist tradition. But the denomination has become somewhat distracted and forgetful of that tradition in recent years. Following World War II, some within the church were counseling the colleges to "go independent." During the tumultuous sixties and seventies, others felt deeply at odds with campus ministries—the church's mission to non-Methodist campuses.

As a result of its unease with ministry in higher education, the church decided to launch an intensive study. In 1973, the National Commission on United Methodist Higher Education was formed. In 1976 it presented its report. Its conclusion: the time had come to rekindle the church's educational commitment, not to abandon it.

Because of that freshened commitment, major changes occurred. The church's colleges were more tightly knit to the church through the Division of Higher Education and the University Senate. The lines of support to campus ministry from the general church were multiplied and strengthened.

But one of the most significant results was the creation of the Annual Conference Board of Higher Education and Campus Ministry. For the first time in many years the church placed its mind and heart together at the center of its programmatic life: the Annual Conference Council on Ministries. Higher education became an essential ministry of the annual conference.

In 1980, for the first time, General Conference mandated that each annual conference have an Annual Conference Board of Higher Education and Campus Ministry. It also made provisions in every local church or charge for a Work Area in Higher Education and Campus Ministry.

The Annual Conference Board of Higher Education and Campus Ministry, therefore, is at a time of new beginnings and of the renewal of a vision. For many Boards, the years since 1980 have been times to discover or create ties to church-related colleges and campus ministries. That has not been an easy task—especially where new lines of administrative authority had to be drawn and budgets have been imperiled.

But this has also been a time to restore United Methodism to its original bright vision of higher education. United Methodists are people with minds to tend as well as hearts to warm. They know (or once knew), also, that the way we tend our minds will determine how we tend this world—God's world—and each other.

What lies ahead is twofold. The task of maintaining and enhancing the annual Conference's program of ministry in higher education presses upon us first. But preparing the way, the way sunlight prepares the way for sight, is the illuminating vision. The Annual Conference Board must understand and display the absolute relevance of higher education, not only to the program of the church, but to its theology, its integrity. It is a high calling.

Benchmarks Along the Way

If the Annual Conference Board is to interpret the church's ministry in higher education, it needs some purchase on the past events that have led up to the present situation. While this is no place for a detailed history, here are some of the historical benchmarks. Together they explain some of the character and personality of our ministry in higher education today.

1. United Methodist higher education bears the impress of both of its historical parents.

The first parent is the Protestant Reformation. That dramatic moment in history centers on Martin Luther's recovery of a New Testament affirmation: "While we were yet sinners, Christ died for us." Faith begins with God's initiative. Humans respond with thanksgiving.

That trust that God acts first and creates new beings, led many of Luther's successors to focus on how humans can express their gratitude. One answer was this: gratitude can be expressed through acts of piety and charity. The impulse, then, was to acts of good will and mercy.

The other parent of Methodism is the Enlightenment. This movement, which influenced French and British thinkers for more than two centuries (A.D. 1700-1900), and shaped the vision of the founders of the United States, wove interestingly through Methodism.

Enlightenment thought places deep trust in the ability of reason. Reason can penetrate the obscurity of myth and the shrouds both crowd and culture place over truth.

For religious persons, the Enlightenment left three important marks. First, a trust that reason, as it understands nature, understands God's handiwork. Therefore, the proper exercise of reason in effect, "thinks God's thoughts after God." Second, a conviction that reason, as it clears away the brush and tangle of prejudice, clears the ground for discovering truth. Therefore, genuine progress is possible in science and in human affairs. And third, a belief that human beings are capable of reason, and therefore educable, and therefore improvable.

If one puts those parents together, one might expect a child who cultivates good works as acts of faith, who labors to educate and improve humankind, and whose own life reflects an energetic curiosity about the world and a belief that the mind can discover remedies for much of what ails it. There was such a child. It was John Wesley.

The movement Wesley began, once transported to the colonies, flourished and created a distinctly American version of the parents' influences: Methodism. Combining evangelism, bookishness, and the booster spirit of the frontier, Methodists built schools and colleges everywhere they went.

2. On American Soil.

Once on American soil, Methodism began to develop guiding intuitions for founding schools and colleges. Two of those have remained to this day.

One is tied up with the word *access*. Like the Enlightenment thinkers, Methodists believed that human beings are endowed with the capacity for reason. They deserve access to opportunities to learn, to overcome the oppressiveness of ignorance.

They also believed that persons deserve access to the fruits of American culture (and Western culture generally). Education offered the means to genuine progress, personal and social.

Therefore, Methodists planted their colleges in remote areas, along the frontier, as well as in urban settings. They built schools faster than they could ever support them. It is one of the least understood marks of that time, that schools formed by the church quickly outstripped the church's ability to support them. Very soon, every school and college simply had to assume responsibility for its own management, staff, and finances. For that reason, Methodist institutions have nearly always been, and are now, church-related but self-governing.

The second intuition guiding Methodists was inclusiveness. That intuition was not equally spread among all, and in some areas, lamentably, Blacks and others were deprived of educational opportunity during most of our country's first century. But even so, many schools and colleges formed in the nineteenth century by Methodists stated in their charters that all persons were welcome regardless of race, sex, or religious persuasion. By the decade after the Civil War, Methodists were among the chief sponsors of education for Blacks and for women. Indeed, the world's oldest degree granting institution for women is Wesleyan College in Macon, Georgia—a United Methodist institution.

3. Public Education.

The federal government began to encourage states to offer public higher education, starting in the 1860s. The Morrow Act, also called the Land Grant College Act, gave states large tracts of land which they could sell. With the proceeds, states established agricultural colleges. That Act, slowly but decisively, changed the face of education in the United States. It also influenced the church's ministry in higher education.

The land grant colleges offered, at first, a vocationally-oriented curriculum. And, in the south, Jim Crow laws kept Blacks from those colleges (although some states chartered Black-only land grant colleges). Methodists supported public higher education. But they also realized the need for choice—choice in kind of curriculum, choice for Blacks, and choice for quality. Therefore, during the last quarter of the nineteenth century they maintained their schools and colleges, and even added a few.

By the end of the first quarter of the nineteenth century, the number of public colleges increased. Their curricula enlarged and varied, on the way to their becoming the highly variegated and departmentalized institutions they are today. And larger numbers of students, including Methodists, attended them.

That led to a significant step in the history of United Methodist higher education. Methodist young people still went in large numbers to their church's colleges. But there were more altogether going to college, and Methodists saw many go to the land grant universities. In the words of one historian, the church soon decided it had to follow its children to college. And it did. In Champaign, Illinois, in 1927, it organized the first Wesley Foundation—Methodism's ministry to students at non-Methodist colleges.

At first, Wesley Foundations simply elaborated the idea of the youth group, but adjusted to meet the needs and schedules of college students. Local churches or districts sponsored them. Often, a congregation near campus housed them.

Following World War II, a second stage of campus ministry evolved. The grief and devastation of the war had created a resolve for unity among Christians. The ecumenical movement captured the imaginations of Christians, wearied over the pain caused by the world's divisions and enthusiastic over the resuscitation of the New Testament teaching that there is "one Spirit, one Church, and one God who is father of us all."

Ecumenical campus ministry was born in the spirit of that belief. In it, several denominations joined to create campus ministry units that expressed the unity of the church rather than its division into denominations. The motive was not pragmatic— those ministries were not formed in order to save each denomination the expense of supporting its own ministry on campus. The motive was theological, and it came at a cost. It required risking resources to the decisions of others. It entailed trust that all Christians on campus would find a place in the ministry, if they wished. It summoned forth belief that, in the secular campus and the divided and compartmentalized world, the unity of the Church provided a needed witness and antidote.

4. A Time of Distancing.

Most of the feeling of distance between the church and the ministry in higher education today extends from events that occurred during the 30 years following World War II. Two events especially, both in essence positive, created negative circumstances for the church.

First, beginning with the G.I. Bill and extending through massive programs of student

4

aid, federal and state governments became key financial players in nearly all of higher education. And their financial role went beyond student aid; they also provided grants to colleges, public and private, for buildings and for programs.

The cloud on the outside of that silver lining had to do with the Constitutional issue of the separation of church and state. When government money went to church-related colleges, was it in effect "establishing" a religion? Colleges, increasingly dependent on government money for meeting their growing expenses, seriously questioned whether they could or should remain so visibly close to the church. And the church wondered as well. Some leaders, in fact, counseled the colleges to spin off from the church. A time of distancing between the church and its college began.

Eventually the courts clarified the role of government funds for church-related colleges. Students at church-related colleges may receive federal and state student aid. Those colleges may also receive other forms of government grants, although not for programs of religion. Further, the colleges cannot require chapel or dogmatic courses in religion, or reflect external denominational control. Many forms of religious expression remain open to the colleges, but those most familiar to parents and others were put in question.

Second, the college population burgeoned. By 1970, nearly half of all Americans were 25 years of age or younger. As the youth population swelled, so did the college population. For the first time in history, enormous masses of youth and young adults congregated together in vast universities.

The combined ebullience and rebelliousness of youth would have been sufficient to destabilize the campus. But to them were added some unfortunate seasonings: racial discord, the assassination of political and religious leaders popular among the young, the depersonalization of computerization, and a tragic war. Galvanized by all of these, college students lashed out against the society that created them.

Although they were seldom instigators, campus ministers found themselves often at the heart of campus protests. Their dominant motif was reconciliation. But to achieve that and other social ministries, they had to win the confidence of the students. That meant being with them, understanding them, and, at times, representing the justice of their causes. Parents did not understand. To them, the church's campus ministers, seen in the midst of the turmoil, were fomenting rebellion against the very congregations and families (and country) that supported them.

That caused the members of the church to feel distant from campus ministry. And it caused campus ministers to distance themselves from the structures of the church.

That distancing has been unfortunate for several reasons. One in particular is that it has caused the church to be absent from one of the more creative efforts of campus ministry. While, for many years, campus ministers have tried to extend a ministry to the whole campus—to embrace student work but to go beyond it to deal with those who create the environment and direction of higher education—since the 1970s that effort has gained strength and sophistication. With its back turned to campus ministry, the church lost both the sight of and the rationale for that movement. It tends instead to fear the revolt of the 1960s and 1970s, yearn for the student work of the 1930s and 1950s, and to feel remote from or puzzled by the 1980s.

The shadows of the three post-World War II decades remain with us.

5. Union.

The Evangelical United Brethren Church and the Methodist Church united in 1972 to form The United Methodist Church. The planning committees for the union had worked for four years to make a new structure that would gather into itself the traditions and the missions of both denominations. Ironically, although both had formed colleges and both offered ministries on campuses, the new structure took precious little account of ministry in higher education in the annual conference and local church.

The *Discipline* made Commissions on Higher Education optional for the annual conference, but not mandated as were Global Ministries, Discipleship, and Church and Society. The structure ignored the connection of local churches and districts with campuses and students.

That oversight allowed the ministry of the newly formed church to shape itself without reference to its historic commitment to higher education. Without consistent representation within the structure of the annual conference, colleges and campus ministries lacked advocates and interpreters. And the church lacked a piece of its mental and missional apparatus.

Fortunately, many conferences jerry-rigged their own structures. But it was not until 1980 that The United Methodist Church made a home for its ministry in higher education at the hearth of the annual conference. It mandated the formation of the Higher Education and Campus Ministry in each annual conference. It also placed a Work Area for Higher Education and Campus Ministry in each local church.

Being a latecomer has challenged those new Boards. But their presence restores United Methodism to its historic commitment to higher learning. The task now is to regain the minds of United Methodists. The Board works in the annual conference, not only to occupy the place designated for higher education, but to display the dimension that higher education adds to everything done by the conference. It is a time of reformation and enlightenment all over again.

Conclusion

It is the gift of the ministry in higher education to brighten the minds, hearts, and hopes of the church. That is done through careful work with and for the church's institutions: schools and colleges, Wesley Foundations and ecumenical campus ministries, and careful attention to church and public issues that affect access and choice in education.

The church needs to learn to hold this gift in its hands with trust and confidence, as it would hold its own soul and essence. For that, ministry in higher education must not only monitor church institutions, it must educate the church. And for that, a strong and steady hand will be required. The Board will have to do its work well. It will teach as well as manage.

Toward those ends, this *Handbook* has been written.

Chapter Two

The Ministry Of The Annual Conference Board Of Higher Education And Campus Ministry

What specifically is the Annual Conference Board of Higher Education and Campus Ministry asked to do? We will deal with the exact statements from the *Book of Discipline* in each of the following chapters. For now, let's try to get the big picture. What does an overall view of the Board's ministry show us?

By way of a general response, the Board is asked to manage the annual conference's ministry in higher education. Certain ministries must be carried out, and the Board is the only one assigned to carry them out. The word *manage* is not used accidently here. It comes from the Latin *manus*, "hand." The Board must take this ministry in hand.

But what is it that the Board is asked to take in hand? One way to answer that is to lay out the broad areas assigned to the Board by the *Discipline*. Those areas define the scope of the mission of the Annual Conference Board of Higher Education and Campus Ministry.

There are two main areas of mission for the Board. The first we can label as its programmatic mission. In that area, the Board extends its ministry to the world. The second is its connectional mission, in which the Board works to strengthen or represent other agencies of the church in their ministry in higher education.

In each area, the Board has three responsibilities.

Programmatic Area	Connectional Area
Campus Ministry	District and Local Church
Schools, Colleges, and Universities	The Annual Conference
Public Policy	The General Church

We'll look briefly at each of these, and then outline some of the management tasks the Board fulfills in its work.

The Programmatic Area

The church reaches out to the world through higher education in a variety of ways. Often it works with and through other agencies. On non-United Methodist campuses it works with campus ministries. But it also works with United Methodist colleges in their ministry to the church and world. And it works with other groups in higher education to shape the state and national policies in higher education. Let's look at each in turn.

Campus Ministry.

Campus ministries will be one of two kinds. Either they will be Wesley Foundations—ministries owned and operated exclusively by The United Methodist Church, or they will be ecumenical—ministries owned in common with one or more other denominations and managed predominantly by their own boards (state or local).

The Annual Conference Board has its fullest responsibility with Wesley Foundations. The Wesley Foundation Boards are accountable to the Annual Conference Board for their missions and ministries, and they must adhere to the Annual Conference Board's policies. In the most direct sense, they are ministries of the Annual Conference Board.

Ecumenical campus ministries have a different posture toward the denomination. Normally, each participating denomination has helped to negotiate a covenant or other agreement which releases much of the direction of the campus ministry to its own governing board. In these cases, the Annual Conference Board is one of the members of the governing board, representing the interests of the annual conference. But in that setting, it must negotiate with its ecumenical partners and abide by common decisions.

Some Annual Conference Boards also support chaplains. The chaplain, however, ministers in the employ of the church-related college. That places chaplaincy within the structure and governance of the college. Because of that, the church distinguishes between chaplains and campus ministers. Campus ministers work under the direct (Wesley Foundation) or indirect (ecumenical) governance of the Annual Conference Board. Chaplains minister within the governance of the university and are accountable to the president or dean of students of the university.

Schools, Colleges, and Universities.

The Annual Conference Board links the annual conference to the schools, colleges, and universities of The United Methodist Church. This ministry divides three ways.

First, most annual conferences have a special relationship to United Methodist schools, colleges, and universities located in or near the annual conference. In many cases, those conferences founded the schools. But many schools were begun by others and then "adopted" into the conference. The Annual Conference Board represents the annual conference in its relationships to those colleges. The scope of that representation differs from conference to conference, and shrinks or dilates depending upon historical circumstance. Nonetheless, in the various ways a conference relates to its "special" colleges, its representative is the Annual Conference Board.

Second, the Board also conveys to the annual conference the opportunities afforded to it by the entire family of United Methodist schools, colleges, and universities. That family includes primary and secondary schools, two-year colleges, four-year liberal arts colleges, universities, graduate professional schools, and theological seminaries. Together they lay out a rich buffet of educational choice, and they offer a fine assortment of financial aid packages. They depend upon the Board to get their message into the minds of United Methodists.

Third, the Board keeps bright before the church the vision of its ministry with historically Black colleges. Eleven Black colleges dwell within the United Methodist family. They continue to offer a unique and potent ministry. Although they receive apportioned funds through World Service, their message still needs telling. The extent of their mission outstrips their financial resources. The Annual Conference Board becomes their friend, their advocate, and their interpreter.

Public Policy.

Most of education today, public or private, relies on federal and state money. Programs of aid to students, programs of grants to institutions, programs of contracts for research and special services—all of those combine to put needed funds into and to stimulate needed activities within American colleges and universities.

Since the G.I. Bill following World War II, the government role in guaranteeing educational opportunity to all deserving citizens has expanded. By 1988, the federal and state governments were investing more than $50 million a year in higher education.

United Methodists support that involvement. Their historic belief in access to education expresses itself there. Their historic belief in choice expresses itself in their support for funding that benefits both private and public colleges. And they know, when bills in state legislatures are voted up or down, the fate of the educational hopes of many rise and fall with them.

The Annual Conference Board provides the conference's focus on public policy issues that affect access, choice, and the public good. It is the educator of the conference and its advocate in the political marketplace. And its eyes are on both the federal and state government as it acts.

The Connectional Area

In its work, the Annual Conference Board does not stand alone. It has the potential for good teamwork with other agencies of the annual conference. The word *potential* is used purposely, because the team needs yet to be oriented and trained for its work. In other cases, the Board itself has not yet had time to fully prepare itself to cooperate with its team members.

That team is part of the connectional life of the church. In this "connectional area," the Board develops the skill and understanding of others who, in turn, can strengthen the ministry in higher education. In most annual conferences, for the time being, the program of the Board will be to get those connectional agencies ready to work. Eventually, the Board will shift its approach and be able to work with and through those agencies.

There are three:

Districts and Local Churches.

Since 1980, the *Book of Discipline* has said that each local church or charge should have a Work Area Chairperson of Higher Education and Campus Ministry. It also allows districts to have Chairpersons or Committees of Higher Education and to place them on the District Council on Ministries. Many have done so. The *Discipline* also names the Annual Conference Board as the link to the districts and local churches—for training and for resources.

In most annual conferences, the number of local churches exceeds by far what an Annual Conference Board could hope to train and resource directly. The necessary tack is to find a way to magnify the effects of its ministry from a point closer in to the local church. In many cases, that "close in magnifier" will be the district.

A District Committee (or Chairperson) of Higher Education and Campus Ministry can accomplish two useful tasks. It can infuse higher education programming into the activities of the District Council on Ministries. And it can gradually extend incentives, activities, and training to local churches. Done right, and with patience, the Board—through its district team—can bring the church's higher education wares to the local church. And it can help the local church discover, no matter where it is, a higher education dimension to its own ministry.

The Annual Conference.

Two aspects of the annual conference should always inform the mind of the Annual Conference Board. The first is the opportunity afforded by the annual meeting of the conference. The second is the necessities arising from the infrastructure of the conference as it goes about its daily work for the remainder of the year.

The Annual Conference Board orchestrates the presence of higher education at the annual meeting of the conference. It manages the routine affairs: the written and oral reports, the presentation of the programs of campus ministries and colleges, and the special drives and emphases.

But it does more than that. It also helps to create the environment of annual conference. Will there be special music? A display? Will recipients of United Methodist loans and scholarships be recognized? The Board plans ways to use the environment of annual conference to broadcast messages about the value of ministry in higher education. In all of these, it cooperates closely with the Conference Planning Committee.

The other aspect of the Board's program in the Annual Conference has to do with the day-to-day life and operation of the Conference. Many other groups affect the quality and quantity of the Board's work. They must be kept informed and inspired by the Board's program and mission. Among these groups are the Cabinet, the Conference Council on Ministries, the Conference Council on Finance and Administration, the Conference Nominating Committee, and the Conference Council staff.

Some conferences also have committees on goals and implementation, long-range planning, and emerging issues. Each of those will need to see the higher education implications of its work—both how higher education, through its colleges and campus ministries, can enhance its work and how its work can strengthen the colleges and campus ministries. The more those committees know about the ministry in higher education, the less the risk that significant decisions will be made in forgetfulness of it.

The General Church.

The *Discipline* names the Annual Conference Board of Higher Education and Campus Ministry as the liaison between the general church and the annual conference, districts, and local churches. The United Methodist Church has several programs that belong to all of its members. It also has resources that can benefit all of its members. In higher education those are placed under the care of the Division of Higher Education of the General Board of Higher Education and Ministry. The Division, jointly with the Annual

Conference Board, takes them to the churches.

Of the church-wide programs, Boards will find themselves working with United Methodist Student Day, United Methodist loans and scholarships, conference academic scholarships, the Black College Fund, the Africa University, the $100 Million Scholarship Fund, and World Communion Sunday. For them all, the General Board of Higher Education and Ministry and United Methodist Communications create promotional materials and program ideas for annual conferences and local churches to use.

In addition, the general church provides grants, resources, and church-wide opportunities in higher education. It can make consultants available, offer advice and counsel, help with training, and direct the Board toward other sources of information. It also offers direction in student ministries and student movements. In some cases, through the Division of Higher Education, it will help with legal issues. For each of these, its essential partner is the Annual Conference Board.

The Tasks of Management

As it goes about its work, the Annual Conference Board will find itself called upon to do many kinds of things. The list below summarizes them. It offers an overview of the sorts of tasks that most often fall to management groups. While each Board will operate somewhat differently, all Boards will carry out some of these tasks some of the time. It is good to think ahead about them.

Before the summary, however, the Board needs to be alerted to a matter concerning its own record keeping. Minutes of meetings are the church's essential memory for mission. With quadrennial changes and personnel shifts, Boards always watch experienced persons depart. If records are not kept carefully and *reviewed* periodically, the Board suffers managerial amnesia.

As a matter of course, each Board ought to review its minutes from 1980 to the present, and isolate every decision made about policy and procedure. The secretary should inscribe those in a Policies and Procedures Handbook, updating it after each meeting. The Handbook then may be duplicated for each member of the Board and should be the tool for orientation of new Board members.

That much said, let us now define briefly policies and procedures and the other management tasks of the Annual Conference Board of Higher Education and Campus Ministry.

Policy.

The word *policy* has it root in the Greek word *polis,* "city" or "state." It grew in meaning to produce the word *politikos,* "citizen of a state." It then branched out more to produce *he politike,* "the art and science of government." And, from there, it extended to our word *police*—our enforcers of the rules and laws of citizenship.

Policies, then, have to do with long-term rules that hold for all. They form the boundaries which define both legitimate and required behaviors.

Annual Conference Boards will set policies, and they will recommend policies to the annual conference. Their policies may govern many things; for example, the fact and manor of evaluation of campus ministries, the standards for conference merit scholarships, the schedule by which reports from colleges and budget requests must be received and reviewed, and much more.

Procedures.

Much of the work of management has to do with figuring out the best procedures for implementing policies. If policies state how things "shall be," procedures tell the steps to take to get and keep them that way.

Procedures prescribe ways to do things. They are more fluid than policies. If one procedure doesn't work, it can be adjusted until it does work.

But the Board will do more than set procedures to carry out its policies. In many areas, the Board may be far from ready to adopt a policy but will still need to devise ways to get work done. Consequently, much of its time will be devoted to crafting procedures. For example, what will be the steps by which church-related colleges will be reviewed, what are the best stages for determining the need for a new campus ministry, how will property needs of Wesley Foundations be determined, how will the Board plan its long-term program, how will the program for annual conference be prepared, and how will the Cabinet and the Conference Council on Ministries receive timely information about the Board's program?

Very few of those items will ever harden into policy. But they will keep the channels clear for the smooth flow of Board work. In general, it is best to deal with all significant issues as matters of procedure first, to find a method of managing them. Then, perfect the method through experience. Finally, if a policy seems needed, establish one.

Program.

The Board exists for the sake of the program of ministry in higher education. Its sights at each meeting ought to be on the quality and range of programming and on how it can energize it. In some cases, the Board provides the administrative support for programs done by others: Wesley Foundation Boards, for example, carry out the ministry on a campus, but the Annual Conference Board provides essential financial, personnel, and property services to keep the ministry strong.

But the Board also has its own program. It promotes the colleges and campus ministries, it evaluates them, it represents its own goals and aspirations for them. It also engages the district and local church higher education chairs, including them in its projects and aiding them as they do their own.

A clue to program lies in the word's roots. *Gramma*, in Greek, meant a letter of the alphabet, or something written. *Pro* means "before." A program, in that early sense, would be a proclamation done before others, literally a proclamation in public. The Annual Conference Board will, at times, invisibly reinforce the visible public ministries of others. It will also, at times, become the visible presence of that ministry.

Personnel.

The Board deals with personnel in many ways. First of all, it organizes its own membership. Second, it can select additional persons to work as advisors, consultants with voice but no vote, representatives, and task group members.

But it has other personnel duties. It sets the policy for the election of Wesley Foundation Board members. It helps determine the procedure for professional staff selection for Wesley Foundations. It plays a role in those cases where annual conferences nominate, elect, or confirm college trustees.

Selection of personnel, particularly professional staff, leads quickly to other personnel concerns. Among them, lines of reporting and responsibility, compensation, evaluation, and continuing education.

Property.

While not all Annual Conference Boards hold property, nearly all have to budget to care for property. The Board, also, by *Discipline*, grants permission to Wesley Foundations to hold property. It consults on legal and property matter with campus ministries and church-related schools and colleges. Usually, its property interests are of four kinds.

First, budgeting for building and maintenance. Wesley Foundations are ministries of the annual conference. Ultimately, their location and condition are conference responsibilities. That does not mean that Wesley Foundations never raise their own funds for building and maintenance. It does mean that the annual conference has a share in the responsibility.

Occasionally annual conferences deed all of their properties over to the conference board of trustees. In that case, the Annual Conference Board must determine which responsibilities fall to the trustees and which to the Board.

In regard to ecumenical campus ministries, the Conference Board handles its responsibility through the ecumenical board.

In most cases, schools and colleges will assume responsibility for the building and maintenance of their own properties. However, annual conferences have often assisted in raising funds to support capital and maintenance campaigns for colleges.

Second, liability. A warning should be sounded here. Colleges and campus ministries tie in to annual conferences in various ways. There is no general rule that tells how liability distributes among them. But one property concern that has required more and more attention is that of ascertaining the degree of legal liability the annual conference bears for its campus ministries and schools and colleges. And it does have the responsibility of making certain that its properties are safe and well insured.

Third, in the event that a church-related college or campus ministry moves to change its relationship with the church, the Annual Conference Board alerts the Division of Higher Education of the General Board of Higher Education and Ministry, so that proper steps can be taken to secure the interests of the church.

Fourth, the Board is asked to see that legal documents are in order pertaining to the campus ministries and schools and colleges of the conference. Are reversionary clauses in their charters? Do they require advice or notice about the rules of the conference or the laws of the state? Do they hold funds in trust from the annual conference? While the Board may not have the expertise itself to carry out these tasks, it does have access to the legal counsel of the annual conference and to other experts.

Promotion.

The Board will also find itself doing promotional work. One task of management is public relations, and the Board will do some of that. But promotion differs from public relations. As the parts of the words imply, *promotion* means moving (motion) forward (pro). Promotion, for our purposes means moving the enterprise forward.

In most cases the promotional question will be: who needs to know (or have) what by when in order to move the enterprise on? That narrows the range. Public relations scattershoots information, relying on the law of averages to collect enough response to make it worthwhile. Promotion gets the right information to the right person at the right time to move things ahead.

Good promotion, then, means asking who needs to know what and by when. It forces managers to ask where the essential pools of information gather and who the key players at various stages are. It then gets that information to the right person in a timely manner. It may be the chair of the Board, it may be the Cabinet representative, it may be a college president, or the Conference Council Director. Those persons all sit in strategic places at strategic times. Their need to know must be met by the Board.

Principal.

Managers have to deal with dollars, with budgets, and with fiscal planning. The *Discipline* directs the Annual Conference Board to assess the needs of the colleges and campus ministries of the conference and to present a budget for their support to the Conference Council on Ministries and the Council on Finance and Administration. In doing that, the Board often assembles the largest program budget in the annual conference.

Whatever funds flow from the annual conference to ministries in higher education, flow through the budget of the Annual Conference Board. That, then, requires the Board to receive a proper accounting of the use of its funds by the colleges and campus ministries it supports.

The Board sets policy about the use of principal, determining, for example, whether funds given to campus ministry must be used for salary or other designated items. It may also direct its gifts to colleges for scholarship or chaplaincy programs. It may also work within the conference to obtain salary guarantees for its campus ministers and to separate wage and benefits from program items in the budget.

The Board may also find ways to earn additional funds to underwrite its ministry in higher education and suggest those to the conference. It could, for instance, seek to establish a Higher Education Foundation for gifts, bequests, and grants to guarantee the longevity of its work against the shrinking of the annual conference budget.

Planning.

Managers plan. This word also has interesting and informative roots. It had, in Indo-European, the meaning "flat" and referred to something, therefore, that was clear and easy to see, and something that was easy to build upon. A plan eventually came to mean, in our terms, a design for taking the wrinkles out of things, for making them easy to build upon.

To do that, managers try to get the clearest sight possible of the future they want and of the resources they will need. In the church, they also try to assess the needs to be met. With those things in sight, they then design the procedures to get to that future. In other words, they plan.

The Annual Conference Board plans for the conference's present and future ministry in higher education. Like all planners, it must determine the future it wants. It must determine the needed resources. It must know the needs it is responding to. And it must clear the way for the work to proceed. Thinking of it as "getting the wrinkles out of the way" is not a bad notion at all.

Conclusion

The Annual Conference Board has areas of work given solely to it. It also has kinds of tasks that it shares generally with all who manage. By experience, it will develop the knack of matching management skills to program area needs. The emphasis, however, is on the phrase "by experience." The Board will have to be active. It will also have to schedule times of reflection to learn from its activities. Then it can make wise policies.

The magnitude of the work at first might seem to exceed the time and talent of any Board. It probably does. The important thing is to go patiently and to learn.

In the pages that follow, we will describe several kinds of programs and identify a multitude of issues in each area. All of them may seem urgent. Nonetheless, it is better to determine what can be done and to begin. Allow in your planning for a growth in responsibility and effectiveness. Plot where you wish to be at the end of this quadrennium and the next. Set your own priorities. That should take some of the wrinkles out.

With that much said, let us now look more carefully at the specific items in the Board's programmatic and connectional areas.

Chapter Three

The Annual Conference Board
And The
Schools, Colleges, And Universities
Of The United Methodist Church

The Annual Conference Board of Higher Education continues the church's historic ministry with its schools, colleges, and universities. In Chapter Two we noted three levels of that ministry. In the first, the Board carries through the conference's program with the schools and colleges that have a special relationship with the conference. The Board also acts as the representative of the interests of the schools and colleges within the annual conference.

On a second level, the Board brings information about the entire family of United Methodist schools, colleges, and universities inside the perimeter of the conference, districts, and congregations. Here the interaction may not have the immediacy it has with institutions within the conference. But it may help high school and college students cross some thresholds not possible for them otherwise. Some ways of doing this will be discussed in the chapter on the district and local church.

The third level is with United Methodism's historically Black colleges. The Board can pave the way for many extraordinary opportunities for these colleges and with them. However, we shall save that discussion for the chapter on programs of the general church.

Among the members of United Methodism's educational family, the thirteen theological seminaries have given long-standing service. But, by general agreement, the Annual Conference Board relinquishes most of the duties of relating to them. Instead, the seminaries work closely with Annual Conference Boards of Ordained Ministry. Ordained ministry and the seminaries share a common agenda in the training of clergy. Those matters seem best worked out among them.

However, the *Discipline* does ask the Annual Conference Board of Higher Education and Campus Ministry to recommend levels of financial support for the seminaries. And, of course, nothing prevents the Annual Conference Board from energetic promotion of them. The more vividly they appear to the church, the more others with theological interests will see them as places for significant learning. And the more the church will grasp the comprehensiveness and adequacy of its entire postsecondary educational program.

This chapter deals with the Annual Conference Board and the schools, colleges, and universities with which it has a special relationship. But, before we get to that, we must clear up an important matter. We must answer the question: What is a United Methodist school or college?

What Is a United Methodist School or College?

Some annual conferences and jurisdictions own United Methodist schools and colleges. Others have agreements and covenants expressing special relationships. Some conferences nominate, elect, or confirm trustees of colleges. In some cases, quotas have been set of annual conference members who must be on the boards of trustees of colleges. Surely any or all of those arrangements would seem to suffice for an institution to call itself United Methodist.

Further, many conferences actually originated colleges, and have held close to them over the decades. Many make major financial commitments to the colleges, for current expenses and for buildings and programs. Some have had vigorous financial campaigns to keep their schools and colleges afloat in financially threatening times. Surely that, too, would seem to suffice for a college to be known as United Methodist.

All of those factors are important. Each contributes to a firm and positive relationship between the college and the church. But by themselves, or all together, they do not make a school or college a United Methodist institution. That decision rests elsewhere and is based on somewhat different criteria.

The United Methodist Church bases its decisions about which educational institutions may call themselves United Methodist with the University Senate. The Senate is the denomination's agency for institutional review and approval. The Senate, nearly a century old, is one of the oldest existing educational advisory agencies in the country. As the *Discipline* puts it, "Approval by the senate is prerequisite to institutional claim of affiliation with The United Methodist Church." (par. 519.1)

What does the Senate base its judgment on? The *Discipline* charges the Senate to review institutions to make certain they have "institutional integrity, well-structured programs, sound management, and clearly defined Church relationships." (par. 1519.3) In addition, the Senate must ascertain that the institutions "maintain appropriate academic accreditation" (par. 1519.4) and must "support the development of institutions whose aims are to address and whose programs reflect significant educational, cultural, social, and human issues in a manner reflecting the values held in common by the institutions and the Church." (par. 1518.2)

The *Discipline* adds two other important paragraphs:

Every effort shall be made by both the Annual Conference and institutions to sustain and support each other, but identification of an institution with The United Methodist Church shall depend upon its approval by the senate. The senate shall provide adequate guidelines and counsel to assist institutions seeking initial or renewed affiliation. (par. 1519.2.)

Only institutions affiliated with The United Methodist Church through approval by the senate shall be eligible for funding by Annual Conferences, General Conference, general boards, or other agencies of The United Methodist Church. (par. 1519.3)

17

In its review of institutions, the Senate interviews bishops, local churches, a representative of the Annual Conference Board of Higher Education and Campus Ministry, and, usually, the district superintendent. That information forms an important part of the nucleus of its review and recommendation. The Senate also responds to inquiries of Annual Conference Boards. But the weight of making the judgment falls primarily on its shoulders.

While this is not the place to go into the history of the Senate nor to display all of the reasons for its assignment, some factors can be usefully mentioned, although only briefly.

First, the Senate brings peers to review colleges. It draws its teams from United Methodist schools and colleges and from among United Methodists who work in other colleges. Its desire is to bring high levels of professional appraisal to the institutions. Historically, United Methodist schools and colleges were asked, first of all, to be top flight educational institutions. That continues.

Second, the Senate has access to the resources of the whole church rather than only those of one region or one conference. Because it can select leaders from a wide stream, it can have confidence that its evaluation teams are objective and appropriate to the institution.

Third, nearly every school and college of The United Methodist Church serves a region more vast than any one annual conference. It affects the larger church, and needs, therefore, review by the larger church.

Fourth, its knowledge of the colleges allows the Senate often to perform a mediating and strengthening role in the relationship between the annual conference and its colleges.

Fifth, the Senate allows for uniformity in the church's assessment and treatment of its colleges. Yet, at the same time, it leaves to each college and annual conference a good deal of latitude to determine how they will live and work together. That invites creativity and conviviality into the mix as church and college prepare their common ministry.

How Does the Annual Conference Board Relate To Its Schools and Colleges?

We noted before that some conferences own educational institutions, some have covenants or chartered agreements, and some share only history and good will. In a number of instances, conferences nominate, elect, or confirm the college's trustees. Members of those boards of trust may, by agreement or by charter, have to include quotas of United Methodists. And, in schools and colleges owned or controlled by the general church, jurisdiction, or annual conference, the *Discipline* requires that three-fifths of the trustees be members of a local church, annual conference, or the Council of Bishops of The United Methodist Church. (par. 2553) That number can be adjusted, but never reduced to less than the majority of members of the board of trustees.

Nonetheless, however the institution's board of trustees gets itself constituted, once it is in place, it assumes complete responsibility for the institution. For reasons of law and of accreditation, that Board must become the final authority for the actions and program of the institution.

A good way to think about the functioning relationship between the Annual Conference Board and the annual conference's schools and colleges is this: they relate to one another as two churches would that are members of the same Conference and have areas of ministry in common. Neither can tie or bind the other. Each has responsibility for its own ministry. Yet, portions of the world will be better served if they act in concert than if they each potter about separately.

Within that broad definition, let us look more closely at how the *Discipline* directs the annual conference in its work with schools and colleges. Following that, several sets of programs and projects will be considered.

The Discipline and the Ministry With United Methodist Schools, Colleges, and Universities

The *Book of Discipline* speaks directly to the Annual Conference Board about its program with schools, colleges, and universities. In this section we will look at each of the paragraphs in which it does. To begin with, the *Discipline* directs the Board:

To interpret and promote the United Methodist ministries in higher education which are . . . specifically related to the Annual Conference. [par 732.4a(1)]

Those schools and colleges, in or near the annual conference, that have a special relationship with the conference, rely upon the Board to keep their story before the church. The colleges have their own public relations efforts. Those, of necessity, have to have broad appeal, for the majority of their students will come from other religious traditions.

The Annual Conference Board, joining forces with the schools and colleges, helps them address their United Methodist constituents. That includes finding ways for congregations to have good, recent information at their fingertips—information on programs, tuition and fees, major awards won by faculty, students, and staff; scholarships; college resources that are available to the annual conference and to local churches; and more.

But promotion also means staying close to the college so that the Board has a current and accurate knowledge of it. In the internal life of the conference (Cabinet, Councils on Ministries and Finance and Administration, Conference Council Staff, for example) issues will arise and attitudes will be formed. They will effect the direction of the conference's finances and affections. Often, the college has no access to those arenas. The Annual Conference Board will stand there in its stead. It will get the right information to the right people at the right time.

To recommend the policies guiding the Annual Conference in its program of ministry in higher education. [par. 732.4a(3)]

Annual conferences may relate to schools and colleges in any of several ways. Initiating those relationships, consulting with the institutions, gathering supporting data, and shaping statements of policy—all are tasks of the Board. Because the schools and colleges must have independent boards of trustees, annual conferences cannot vote to set policies for them. But they can, and must, help set the policies that guide their own relationships to the schools and colleges.

Policies may have to do with such things as these (depending upon local charters and covenants): budget requests from the college, election and/or confirmation of trustees for the college, use of conference generated scholarship or program funds, and use of the program apparatus of the annual conference by the college for the purpose of fund raising and recruiting. The college will have its policies as well. The conference will need to respect those and to work in a spirit of cooperation for the benefit of both.

To provide counsel, guidance, and assistance to United Methodist schools, colleges, and universities regarding their relationship to the state. [par. 732.4a(4)]

In most cases, schools and colleges will have their own legal consultants. Further, their boards of trustees will normally assume responsibility for operating within the boundary of state law. Yet, there may be peculiarities stemming from the college's church-relatedness that affect its legal status. For example, if the annual conference is the corporation for the college, that may affect the state's interpretation of liability.

More likely than giving counsel to the college will be assistance to the college on matters of joint concern. An example has to do with the recent interest of governments in finding fresh sources of tax revenue. That search has led assessors and others to challenge previously tax exempt church (and church-related) institutions. Within the past few years, second parsonages of congregations have come under scrutiny, as have theaters and sports arenas of colleges. In these cases, when the brush will likely spread wide and cover many, conference and college may need to work together to discover where equity lies. They may then move in common cause.

To represent the Annual Conference in its relationship to United Methodist schools, colleges, and universities, especially those related to the Annual Conference. [par. 732.4a(5)]

The *Discipline* makes it clear that the Annual Conference Board is the conference's representative to its schools and colleges. The obverse of that holds, as well. The Board is the college's conduit to the annual conference.

Conferences ought to respect the good economy of this paragraph. It locates the channel through which the college moves on its way to approaching any other agency of the annual conference. With that routine comes the assurance that appropriate persons will always be alerted to what is happening.

Colleges also do well within that economy. Rather than dealing with separate expectations from near and far-flung groups within the conference, they have one clearly identified representative agency to know and work with.

The Board, then, will orchestrate the college's presence at the yearly gathering of the annual conference, will carry its ideas and programs to the Council on Ministries, and keep districts and local churches informed. Other conference agencies will make their interests and questions known to the college through the Board.

To present to the Council on Ministries and then to the Council on Finance and Administration of the Annual Conference the financial needs for adequate support of the schools, colleges, theological schools . . . related to the Annual Conference for allocations of apportionments to the churches within the conference. [par. 732.4a(10)]

The Board prepares the conference's higher education budget. It must assess the financial needs of the conference's schools and determine what portion of them ought to be met by the conference. All budget requests from the colleges ought to come through the Board's budget. The colleges should have a place in the yearly budget of the conference. When colleges sponsor special askings or drives which require the conference's permission or seek a place in the conference budget, the Annual Conference Board will represent them and help the college take its case to the conference.

Notice that in the *Discipline,* the Board is directed to take its budget to two agencies. Most of the program Boards of the conference take their budgets only to the Council on Ministries. Not so for Higher Education and Campus Ministry. The reasons for this will become clearer in the chapter on campus ministry. But even with the colleges there is a reason.

The school or college tends to use its money from the Conference for scholarships, chaplain's programs or salaries, or in its general budget to cover instructional salaries. Those kinds of expenses fall outside the usual definition of conference program expenses. While the budget for the program of the Annual Conference Board ought to merge with the entire program budget of the Council on Ministries, its budget covers more than program. Because it does—covering expenses for college scholarships and salaries—at least that part of its budget should receive a hearing in the Council on Finance and Administration. That is usually the place where salary and administrative budgets and policies receive their hearing.

To counsel United Methodist schools, colleges, universities . . . related to the Annual Conference with regard to their charters and constitutions, reversionary clauses, and liability. [par. 732.4a(17)]

To counsel United Methodist institutions about property and endowments entrusted to the institutions and to maintain and enforce trust and reversionary clauses in accordance with the provisions of the Division of Higher Education under 1516.3c. [par 732.4a(18)]

To monitor fiduciary and legal relationships with United Methodist schools, colleges, and universities . . . and to assist Annual Conferences in their responsibilities in these matters. [par. 732.4a(19)]

The United Methodist Church encourages all institutions that are owned by the church or that have benefited substantially from their relationship to the church, to include a reversionary clause in their charters. While the specific wording of the clause should have the benefit of legal counsel, the spirit of the document should be clear. In the event the institution closes, what has been given to it in the interests of furthering the church's mission in higher education should return to the church.

Other things to bear in mind about institutional charters are these: The charter must clearly spell out the relationship of the institution to the church. It, or the constitution of the school or college, will detail precisely what portion (if any) of the board of trustees will be United Methodist. And the charter must be drawn in a way that protects the conference and the college from legal liability for each other in the event of financial loss or litigation.

Also, when there are specific properties, endowments, or trusts made to schools and colleges on behalf of the church, the Annual Conference Board must keep a record of them, keep the institutions aware of them, and enforce the reversionary clause in the event the institution closes or changes its relationship to the church.

There will also be times when, for good reason, schools and colleges must change their charters. In some cases, that change must receive the approval of the annual conference. It may also require review by the conference's legal counsel. The Annual Conference Board will monitor the process of charter change and will represent the interests of the annual conference. It will also find ways, in cooperation with the college, to protect the separate interests of each.

To evaluate schools, colleges, universities . . . of the Annual Conference with concern for the quality of their performance, the integrity of their mission, and their response to the missional goals of the General Church and the Annual Conference. [par. 732.4a(20)]

Colleges are complex organisms. It probably lies beyond the resources of the Annual Conference Board to evaluate their total programs. In fact, that is not necessary. The regional accrediting agency certifies the adequacy of the educational offering. The University Senate certifies general compliance with the expectations of the church.

What then does this paragraph ask the Annual Conference Board to do? First, to know the program of the college and to ascertain that it is of high quality. That can be done by discussing with the president or church relations officer whether the institution is fully accredited, whether it has been asked by its regional agency or the University Senate to address certain problems, and whether the institution's own self-review has revealed the need for change and strengthening.

The point of this questioning is not adversarial. The Board, however, should not be the last to know of the problems of the institution. It is often in the best position to head off rumors and other mischief but it must know the facts ahead of time. Usually, the Board will seek information as a part of its effort to support the institution, and to show the church how its support keeps the college vital and competent.

Second, the Board is asked to know the mission of the school or college. Regional accrediting agencies expect each institution to have a mission statement. They measure the appropriateness of the college's programs and plans by asking how they match the college's stated mission. That mission statement becomes the Board's best tool for explaining the college to others.

A more difficult assignment will be to help the college find ways to respond to the missional goals of the general church and annual conference. The financial resources of most colleges are slim. Their regional accrediting agency expects the institution's energy to be spent fulfilling its stated mission. Further, the college's trustees must assume responsibility for guiding the institution according to its own mission, not according to another.

That much said, there still remains broad terrain on which the church and the college have common interests. The Board ought to discuss conference and church goals with the college yearly. At that time, the college and the Board can identify areas of mutual interest. For example, colleges share the conference's desire to increase the number of people of color in the student body, the faculty, and the staff. They also have experts in a number of areas who can consult with the conference, assist with research on conference programs, train conference leaders in fund raising or development techniques, and provide the setting for meetings and convocations addressing the missional goals of the conference. The Annual Conference Board should enable that kind of cooperation to occur. And it should be aware when it has not.

To confer at once with representatives of the General Board of Higher Education and Ministry to determine what resources and aid the board may be able to provide and to enable the Division of Higher Education to carry out its responsibilities in the event any educational institution. . . moves to sever or modify its connection with the Church or violate the rules adopted by the division in accordance with par. 1516.3. [par. 732.4a(21)]

Paragraph 1516.3 of the *Book of Discipline* directs the Division of Higher Education to "Take such action as is necessary to protect or recover resources, property, and investments of The United Methodist Church, or of any Conference, agency, or institution thereof, in capital or endowment funds of any educational institution . . . organized, developed, or assisted under the direction or with the cooperation of The United Methodist Church should any such institution move to sever or modify its connection with the Church or violate the terms of any rules adopted by the board or any terms of any such grant of new capital or endowment funds made by The United Methodist Church or any Conference, agency, or institution." The paragraph authorizes the Division to audit and investigate records, and review all documents of institutions that the Division judges to be related to The United Methodist Church.

If a church-related school or college is preparing to alter or sever its tie to the church, paragraph 1516.3 also directs the Annual Conference Board, the bishop, and the institution's trustees and administration to confer with representatives of the Division of Higher Education "at the earliest possible opportunity . . . to determine what resources and aid the division may be able to provide and to permit the division to carry out its responsibilities under this paragraph."

Any change in the relationship of a school or college to the church is freighted with meaning. The implications are not only legal, but educational and communal. It reflects not only an alteration in the status of the institution, but an excision from the heart of the church as well. The Annual Conference Board's first desire, of course, is to work closely enough with its institution that severance does not become an issue. But if that cannot be accomplished, protection of the church's resources and of the college's integrity become paramount issues. For that, the Division of Higher Education and the University Senate are necessary resources.

Not every event signaled under the paragraph has to do with severance. Institutions also modify their relationships with the church. This may be done by rewriting a charter and stating the ties to the church differently. It may be accomplished by adjusting the number of trustees the church elects, or by no longer having the conference confirm elected trustees. Then again, the Conference Board should make contact with the bishop, the college administration, and the Division of Higher Education. It is important, in the case of schools and colleges that have had a healthy historic tie to the church, for the Board to find out first if the institution itself has already initiated contact with the Division of Higher Education. In most cases, they will have done so. In that event, the Conference Board may act as a helpful resource to the institution, and as an interpreter of its new posture to the conference.

In addition to these, which might be thought of as legal or administrative aspects of the Annual Conference Board's with schools and colleges, the *Discipline* offers programmatic instructions as well. Together they provide a useful recipe for activating ministry with, or on behalf of, them.

To make known to the district, subdistrict, and all local churches the names and location of all United Methodist educational institutions and, wherever possible, provide resources interpreting their work and special missions. [par. 732.4b(1)]

The Division of Higher Education provides quantities of free materials to help the Board spread the word about every United Methodist school and college. Its quadrennial publication *College Bound* describes them all: theological seminaries, universities, colleges (four-year and two-year), and preparatory and elementary schools. It tells place, cost, courses, degrees offered, entrance requirements, and more. It also provides complete instruction for obtaining United Methodist loans and scholarships. In addition, it summarizes federal and other aid sources for students.

Brochures with maps of the colleges and mailing addresses are available in quantity free. In addition, colleges have posters, brochures, and information sheets. Some may send staff to the conference to meet with prospective students.

The Board can use these and other means at its disposal to get into the library of every district and local church information about the entire educational offering of the church. Usually, it will come as a surprise to church members when they see the wealth of resources available, and the number of low price, high quality programs provided by church colleges. It will also please them to see, among the church's colleges and universities, many of national reputation and regard.

The point here, however, is to awaken in local church families an awareness that the church has an educational home for them. For that, the information must come systematically and during times when college decisions are being made. Fall and early winter are excellent choices.

To assist institutions related specifically to the Annual Conference in their efforts to raise funds, scholarships, recruit students, and extend services to the Annual Conference. [par. 732.4b(2)]

In recent years the number of United Methodist students at United Methodist institutions has grown. One reason: the efforts of the colleges to make a church-related education available. One index of that effort can be seen by comparing the price of those colleges with other private colleges. In general, private colleges cost their students about six thousand dollars more per year than public institutions. On the average, however, United Methodist colleges cost only three thousand more.

The colleges then go on to fill that gap of three thousand dollars by raising scholarship funds. The Annual Conference Board can support that effort by adopting its own academic or other scholarship programs, by encouraging local churches to create scholarship funds for their members, and by keeping the conference budget item for colleges as high as possible relative to the capabilities of the conference.

Many Boards have launched capital funds campaigns for their colleges. Others have chosen to raise money to underwrite specific programs in colleges. In some conferences, every local church celebrates a special Sunday by recognizing its schools and colleges and by taking an offering.

The Board can be especially useful to colleges by doing three additional things. First of all, by encouraging as many students as possible to consider attending their church-related college. The Conference Councils on Youth and Young Adult Ministries are wonderful allies for programs alerting students to the programs and possibilities at those institutions. In newsletters and at meetings, encourage pastors to tell students to speak directly to the staff at the colleges. Many think they cannot afford a church college, only to find out that the grants and aid offered by the college bring the actual expense far below the catalog price.

Second, the Board can help the college find individual donors. A very high proportion of all charitable giving is done by individuals. Most congregations have persons who can support several charitable causes. Boards that encourage pastors to share names of donors with colleges, help the students, help the church, and help the colleges.

Finally, the Board can help the college extend its services to the church. Colleges usually have tight budgets. But their personnel and services can be freed up for limited projects. College business staff, religion faculty, computer experts, demographers and researchers, and many others, could serve conference needs. But the college needs to know, and so does the conference. The Board is the critical link.

To assume responsibility, after consultation with the Annual Conference Committee on Nominations and the nominating committee of the institution's Board of Trustees, for the nomination of those trustees who are to be nominated and elected by the Annual Conference to the Boards of trustees of United Methodist schools, colleges, and universities. In the event the Annual Conference confirms or elects trustees nominated by trustee-nominating committees, to consult with those committees, having special concern for the selection of persons who will appropriately address the financial, missional, and educational progress of the institution. [par. 732.4b(3)]

The majority of United Methodist institutions nominate and elect their own boards of trustees. But in several areas, annual conferences play a role in the process. The four most common roles are these: 1) nominating some or all trustees and electing some or all; 2) nominating trustees which are then elected by the institution; 3) electing trustees nominated by the institution; or 4) confirming trustees that have been nominated or elected by the institution.

Only since the 1988 *Book of Discipline* has the church made the Annual Conference Board a participant in those processes. If the conference nominates trustees, the Annual Conference Board consults with the trustees' nominating committee and with the Conference Committee on Nominations, and then "assumes responsibility" for those nominations.

In cases where the conference does not nominate, but does elect or confirm candidates named by the institution's trustees, the Annual Conference Board consults with the board of trustees. The Annual Conference Board reviews the proposed slate, with an eye toward finding persons who will strengthen the institution in its mission, its educational program, and its finances.

Here is a list of duties carried out by trustees of educational institutions which was prepared by John W. Nason for the Association of Governing Boards of Colleges and Universities, and is reprinted here with its permission:

1. to appoint the president
2. to support the president
3. to assess the president's performance
4. to clarify the mission
5. to approve long-range plans
6. to approve the educational program
7. to insure financial solvency
8. to maintain the physical plant
9. to preserve institutional autonomy
10. to enhance the public image
11. to serve as a court of appeal
12. to be informed
13. to assess their own performance

In addition, when the conference is invited to help select trustees, it will also consider these duties:

1. to understand and love The United Methodist Church
2. to view positively the church's history and mission in higher education
3. to know the people and the goals of the annual conference
4. to understand and advocate the church's need for its institutions
5. to be willing to work with the church to organize its support of the colleges

A further dimension of the Board's work has to do with connecting the trustees to the annual conference. The Board may know of conference members who would serve the school or college well. Those suggestions are always appropriate. The Board could also invite at least one trustee who is related to the annual conference to serve as a member of the Annual Conference Board. That keeps lines of communication open, and assures the Annual Conference Board of current information about the college for purposes of promotion.

To provide for interpretation of the programs of United Methodist schools, colleges, and universities throughout the educational program of the Annual Conference, and especially in cooperation with those committees and persons responsible for youth and young adult ministries. [par. 732.4b(4)]

While colleges and universities now reach many more "older" students, they still concentrate on youth and young adults. Statistically, those who enter college immediately from high school have the best chances of completing their education. And those who enter within six years of high school graduation have a better chance of adjusting and of completing their schooling within four years.

In the annual conference, those potential students have two programming centers: the Council on Youth Ministries and the Council on Young Adult Ministries. The Annual Conference Board can work directly with those Councils, discovering places and ways to get information about schools and colleges to youth and young adults. Colleges can provide settings for retreats. They can offer resources for special weekend events. They can also work with the two Councils to offer college fairs and other programs that help persons make college choices. And don't overlook the vocational and educational counseling the colleges can offer to potential students. Those, and many other projects, can help the colleges and the students find each other.

The Board may also decide to work in conjunction with the entire Council on Ministries. Almost every program of that Council could have a higher education dimension. Certainly the schools and colleges have useful and interesting resource persons. Celebrations in the conference could feature college choirs or drama groups. Parents' programs could benefit from the college's psychology or home economics staff. Administrative needs of the Council could be refined by consulting with the college business staff. Social concerns projects might gain in dimension and appeal with the background and knowledge of the political science or sociology staff. The possibilities go on from there.

The key for this is to remember that the best interpretation of the college's program comes from fruitful interaction with the college and its staff and students. Good ties and beneficial relationships speak for themselves.

To interpret systematically to the districts, subdistricts, and local churches the conference program with United Methodist schools, colleges, and universities, encouraging their support and participation. [par. 732.4b(5)]

This will be dealt with more fully in the chapter on working with districts and local churches. But for our purposes here, the key words here are *systematically* and *encouraging*. The Annual Conference Board needs a system and a routine for interpreting the schools and colleges. One angle of that has to do with establishing a calendar of events to do each year. On that calendar should be dates for annual mailings of brochures, for obtaining the names of high school juniors and seniors to send to the colleges, for getting *College Bound* to each pastor, for sending a copy of the catalogs from colleges related to the conference to each congregation, for getting posters with tear-off application slips to each pastor, for holding college fairs, for getting a college representative to youth and young adult rallies, for motivating churches to support special Sundays for their colleges. Once on the calendar and in the hands of a committee of the Board, a system has been developed, one that steadily nudges the benefits of the college into the consciousness of the church.

The other word is *encourage*. The word actually means to "cause courage," not simply to urge. And courage itself comes from the word for heart. That's helpful. The Board is to "give heart" to the church about its schools and colleges. If they take the institutions to heart, congregations will participate in and support them. The Board, by bringing the programs of the college to the church (showing how the college works to fulfill the mission and the dreams of people in the church) helps that happen. Encouragement means more than speaking words about the institutions. It suggests engaging the people from the college and church with each other.

Programs With Schools and Colleges

Much of the program done with schools and colleges will grow out of the friendship and mutual interests established between them and the Annual Conference Board. In fact, the most important program of all is the establishment and enhancement of that friendship. With it, many things become possible.

Here are two annotated lists of items that the conference and its colleges might consider together. The first contains expectations that are often on the mind of the church. The second contains topics that are of importance to the colleges. Your lists may differ, but these may at least define a starting line.

1. What does the church expect from its colleges?

Scholarships. United Methodists want assurances that qualified United Methodist students can go to their church's colleges. Most of the colleges already spend more in scholarships for United Methodists than they receive from the annual conference. And many of them wish to see their number of United Methodist students increase.

The Annual Conference Board can encourage the college in those activities. It can also get a detailed list of scholarships and other student aid from the college to share with the church. It should also assist the schools and colleges in finding donors whose gifts will strengthen their scholarship programs.

Leadership. The college has a wealth of specialized leadership. The church tends to be full of generalists. They need each other. One criticism often leveled by the church is that colleges only come around when they want money. The other side of that problem remains unspoken: the Church does not yet know how to seek and use the resources of the college.

The annual conference needs leadership, both for ongoing programs and for special activities. The college that is kept informed about the conference's needs may well have people or equipment available to fit those needs. The conference needs leadership. The college has some. The Board helps put the two together.

28

Some leadership areas in which the college might help the conference are these: financial programs, research, religious life programs, musical and dramatic events, business methods, marketing support, family life programs, educational training for Sunday school teachers, public policy issues, managerial counsel, and buildings and maintenance.

Hospitality. Many colleges host church events. But they need to be more aggressive and imaginative in their efforts to bring people to campus. Study days, retreats, youth weekends, United Methodist Women's programs, United Methodist Men's rallies, youth career days, senior citizens special events, temporary or permanent facilities for episcopal or district offices—any of those extends the welcome mat and gives the church a sense of belonging with the college.

The college also needs to know how important it is for college staff to meet and greet visitors. The small amount of time spent with guests by the president, vice president, chaplain, or church-relations officer makes the visit personal. It assures visitors that this is an institution where people take time for people. Perhaps no message is more important when choices about college are made.

Intellectual Faithfulness. The church wants students at its colleges to challenge and enhance their faith. It wants the scholarly study of religion, and wishes it as rigorous as good scholarship demands. But it also wants to know that the college nests itself and its programs in its affection for the church. To feel that a college is destructive of or indifferent to the Christian faith is to lose faith in the college.

A college is intellectually faithful to the church when its scholarship is intact and first rate, and when it provides an environment in which the Christian faith is honored and supported. That can be done through student religious life groups, through interdisciplinary courses that deal with questions of ethics, through programs for preseminary students, through some courses of service to the church (such as Christian Education), and through attention to the faculty of the college (not that all must be either United Methodist or Christian, but that all deal respectfully with the religious traditions and beliefs of the students).

Good Citizenship. Churches nearby colleges form many opinions about them from observing their local citizenship. Because colleges reach far beyond their local setting in search of students, they are sometimes unaware of their local image. But that image has a way of spreading far beyond local borders. Boards do well to talk with colleges about their local citizenship.

Does the college staff relate to the neighboring churches? Does it take responsibility for its students and take care for their relationship to the city or town? Does the college encourage its employees to become active in civic projects? Does the college work actively with its neighborhood to maintain a healthy and safe environment?

In many ways, colleges serve communities. They provide a needed financial base in many smaller towns. Some are the principal employers and financial mainstays in their locale. Consequently, their public demeanor is observed by many.

2. What do colleges expect from the church?

Students. Of the many things a church-related college is, one of the most important is a community for students. Educational institutions exist for students. And they exist to create among students a community of learning and of mutual responsibility. By sending its students to church-related colleges, the church places the fundamental ingredient onto the campus.

Learning goes beyond honing a keen intellect. College communities teach students responsibility for the quality of life—theirs and others. They encourage the responsible intellect—students taking their share in the communal search for truth but also striving to discover and be true to their own selves. Such learning requires a critical mass of students.

For other reasons as well, the colleges desire students from the church. One is simply the economics of college life. The more students, the more tuition income. The more tuition income, the better the program that can be offered. The better the program, the more benefit the church and others receive from the college's graduates.

The college expects the church, especially the Annual Conference Board, to help United Methodist families look further than the "catalog price" of the college. In fact, private, not-for-profit colleges give more financial aid than any other colleges. Their students also qualify for state and federal aid. But the colleges want the chance to work with students to make a church-related education possible. First and foremost, they want to serve students.

Interpretation. All colleges have mission statements. Those statements are the magnetic north toward which all of their activities aim. Those statements define the college. Annual Conference Boards that know those statements can speak more aptly about the institutions and be better reporters of their faithfulness.

But colleges also need persons not in their employ to talk about the quality of life and learning on campus. When academic prizes are won, when students do community or world service, when new programs are initiated, it appears self-serving when the college broadcasts those events. In fact, if it is a church-related college, those victories belong to the church as well. The Annual Conference Board can present the college's victories with joy and a sense of joint ownership. That message is not likely to be missed.

The colleges also need help interpreting the peculiar animal they are. The college is not a church. It is a liberal arts institution related especially to the church. But it has numerous other constituencies it must satisfy. Other students, faculty, accrediting associations, alumni, donors, federal and state governments, state and national associations, and sometimes unions or other federations of workers or teachers. That means, simply in the course of things, every expectation of the church will not have priority. That does not indicate faithlessness, but the realities of maintaining a college in today's society. The college will need the Board to help United Methodists understand its circumstances and good will at times when its decisions may displease some members of the church.

Access to Finances. Mission and commitment drive the college. But it is fueled by funds. On the average, United Methodist colleges receive slightly less than 2 percent of their operating budgets from the institutional church. That amount matters for material and symbolic reasons. It does help provide scholarships or pay for significant programs. And it indicates something about the identity of the church—that it does view itself as a college-related church.

It may be possible for conferences to enlarge their apportioned offerings to the colleges. The Board should always hold that challenge before the church. But conferences can also include the colleges in their lists of suggestions to persons who are writing their wills and making bequests. Boards can also help locate potential donors in congregations. And they can sponsor special college days. We have already mentioned congregational scholarships; to those we may add congregational endowments for special chairs in departments of religion.

Where conferences themselves can not increase their own support of colleges, they can pave the way for those who can.

Access to Churches, Districts, and the Annual Conference. Many activities in congregations, districts, and annual conferences would have added luster and depth if they could include the resources of church-related colleges. Many colleges would fare better if they had access to those groups. The Board can open the door both ways.

The Board, by careful planning, can guide the college to those pivotal places in the church. Colleges need to know:

- which groups in the conference are natural audiences for their interpretive and promotional programs,
- who the leaders of strategic groups and committees are,
- how to get on the calendar of the annual conference,
- which topics and approaches are best for each group,
- how to implement programs, with the Board and through the Districts and local churches.

The Board also draws up the game plan for the meeting of annual conference. Often the college makes a brief presentation, a speech, or a thank you. Occasionally it makes a financial appeal. The Board now orchestrates the college's place at annual conference and should use its knowledge of the conference to help the college make more memorable and effective use of its time.

Some conference colleges have recruited persons in each local church or charge to represent them. Annual Conference Boards may cooperate in that effort, and supplement the training of those representatives. Each may then, with the pastor's approval, assume the fuller duties of work area Chairperson for Higher Education and Campus Ministry.

The Board can also work with the colleges and with districts to do college fairs— events in which teens, their parents, and representatives of colleges meet to discuss how to choose a college, how to fund a college education, what to expect at college. At those times, students can also talk with college admissions officers to discuss admissions standards and financial aid.

Information. Colleges need accurate information about the atmosphere in the annual conference. If some needs have been identified, some hopes awakened with regard to the college, the college wants to know. In the event of significant complaints, the college needs to know.

The Annual Conference Board, or one of its committees, should meet with the senior staff of the college at least once a year to discuss the higher education climate in the conference. How is the college seen? How is it trying to be seen? The Board or its committee may wish to help the college president set up a President's Council, made up of lay- and clergy persons, as an informal college-relations group. That group can share information, test new ideas for church-relations programs, and provide needed clarity in both circles.

Colleges might also be asked to consider setting up a Church-Relations Committee or Subcommittee of their board of trustees. That would allow for regular review of the college's connection with the church. The Annual Conference Board might also consider inviting a trustee to serve on the Board as an ex officio member. That formalizes a route for information and for partnership, but also respects the distinctions between the two.

Conclusion

The Board, in its work with the colleges:

- represents the conference to the colleges,
- represents the colleges to the conference,
- carries out the provisions of the *Book of Discipline.*

The Board, in that work:

- interprets the work of the college,
- arranges for opportunities for the college to interact with the church,
- arranges for the conference's financial support of the college,
- assures good communication between church and college.

The Board, as a part of its program, also:

- encourages students to attend church-related colleges,
- locates potential donors,
- informs students and families of financial aid programs available through the college,
- helps the church discover ways higher education institutions can add substance to church programs.

Chapter Four

The Annual Conference Board
And The
Campus Ministries Of The Church

The United Methodist Church has ministered to students on non-Methodist campuses for more than half a century. Most campus ministries have been in place much longer than the Annual Conference Board. Many have become well established presences on their campuses.

As the church's campus ministry has evolved, it has tended to take one of four shapes. Understanding those shapes will inform the Board's perspective as it works with those ministries.

Wesley Foundations are campus ministries owned and operated by The United Methodist Church. They are denominational presences on non-United Methodist campuses, and ones that relate most directly to the Annual Conference Board. Roughly half of all United Methodist campus ministries (about 450) are Wesley Foundations.

Ecumenical campus ministries occur when two or more denominations jointly own and operate a ministry on campus. Usually a covenant or contract has been drawn that commits the denominations to support the enterprise and gives the board of the ecumenical campus ministry a good deal of control over the operation of its program. In some cases, contracts or covenants are drawn for each separate ministry; in others, a state ecumenical committee or commission manages the local units, and the covenant is with the state committee or commission.

Cooperative campus ministries fall between Wesley Foundations and ecumenical campus ministries. A ministry is cooperative when a Wesley Foundation board is in place, but the ministry itself shares staff, budget, program, or property with one or more other denominations. The key here is the existence of a Wesley board. So long as that board exists, the ministry must operate within the boundaries and policies that hold for any Wesley Foundation. Its sharing with other denominations follows from the approval of the Annual Conference Board.

Local church and district campus ministries sometimes arise completely independently of the Annual Conference Board. In the case of the district, the funds may come from the annual conference program budget, and the Annual Conference Board may wish to work with the conference Council on Ministries to unify those ministries under the Annual Conference Board.

In the case of the local church, the critical factors have to do with funds and initiative.

If the Annual Conference Board funds the campus ministry of a local church even in part, the program is fully accountable to the Annual Conference Board. It is then a program of the annual conference. If the initiative has come from the Annual Conference Board, some degree of negotiated joint responsibility should be achieved. If the program is locally initiated and funded, it remains simply the program of the local church.

A Model for Managing the Campus Ministry Program

We'll look more carefully at those ministries later in this chapter. For now, it will help to think about one aspect of the Board's work: managing this varied program. Let's begin with drawing on a more familiar source for a model.

The model comes from the local church. Many congregations have created two distinct groups to make certain their ministry is effective. One group cares for the church's administrative work, the other for its program.

The administrative group is the Administrative Board. That Board has oversight of the entire congregation. In it are the chief administrative committees: finance, trustees, pastor/parish, and personnel and nominations. With those committees in place, the church has prepared itself to handle its personnel, property, and budget. In addition, the Administrative Board can establish the policies and the goals for the congregation and review its progress.

However, the Administrative Board has one more ingredient, one without which the rest of the enterprise would be futile: the Council On Ministries. That Council does the program. Under its wing are the congregation's worship, education, stewardship, mission, and social ministries. The Council develops the congregation's missional and programmatic life.

This division of labor is important. When the Administrative Board functions well, it frees the Council on Ministries to do the program. When the Council does its work well, it gives purpose and energy to the work of the Administrative Board. And, of course, the Board must direct, approve, and adopt the program initiated by the Council on Ministries.

Now, apply this model to the Annual Conference Board of Higher Education and Campus Ministry. Of course, like any jacket made for another person, it won't fit perfectly. But it does cover a lot and in a useful way.

First, with Wesley Foundations the model fits best. Wesley Foundation Boards can be thought of as Councils on Ministries. The Annual Conference Board matches the Administrative Board of the local church: it is ultimately responsible for property, personnel, finance, policies, and goals. Further, it must approve, adopt, and evaluate the program of the Wesley Foundation. But the Wesley board is the Council on Ministries—its efforts must invent, inspire, and drive the program on campus. In that, it is like the local church Council on Ministries.

Even in the case of the Wesley Foundation, however, the model needs adjustment. Most annual conferences have more than one Wesley Foundation. Further, those Foundations are strewn about the conference, and are not in one tidy place as in the local church. Therefore, the Annual Conference Board will find itself needing to transfer some parts of its administrative work to the Foundations, simply because those functions require someone close at hand.

Which functions will be transferred? Four will. And only in part. But before we name them, one important point must be made: even when functions are transferred, the ultimate responsibility for their fulfillment remains with the Annual Conference Board. If, by policy, the Board grants certain powers to the local ministry, the policy belongs to the Board, and it remains accountable for it.

With that clarified, what administrative tasks will need to be shared with the Wesley board? Number one is finance. The Wesley board will have to administer its day-to-day budget, make decisions about dispersals, and sometimes about local fund raising. In some ministries, that includes setting salaries for nonprofessional staff members and a variety of other items. Exactly which ones will be determined by the Annual Conference Board. However the lines get drawn, certain financial tasks will have to be delegated to the Wesley board.

Number two is property. Unless otherwise provided for in your conference bylaws, ultimate responsibility for Wesley property falls to the Annual Conference Board. Yet, much care and maintenance of property must be done locally. It is simply too inconvenient to handle them any other way. Purchases of routine items, minor repairs, supplies, equipment—all must be monitored by someone close at hand. Here the Annual Conference Board must decide at which point matters rise above local control and require Board action or approval.

Number three is elected and nonprofessional personnel. The election of Wesley Foundation board members must be done according to policies set by the Annual Conference Board. [par. 732.4c (7)] But, in fact, those local Boards know the local people best. Some arrangement must be made that ensures the array of people and the order of nomination that fits the Board's policies, but that allows the local people maximum voice in selecting interested and qualified members. The same has to do with hiring and working with nonprofessional staff in the Wesley Foundation. The general policies belong to the Annual Conference Board. But the job description, selection, and supervision may be done best by a local committee.

Number four is professional personnel. The *Discipline* clearly places policy responsibility in the hands of the Annual Conference Board. [par. 732.4c(4)] It also makes that Board the principal player in determining the professional leadership for Wesley Foundations. But it also requires consultation with the local board. Further, decisions have to be made in the daily stream of events in the local ministry. Arranging vacations, finding substitutes, giving counsel and advice, setting personal goals, arranging honest feedback about the effectiveness of the staff person—those and other needs are best answered to locally and within the given powers of the Wesley board. Of course, any of them might become problematic and could then become the business of the Board. But, in general, other than the process of securing and evaluating professional staff, the local board might be the best place for the responsibilities of caring for professional personnel. That board, then, reports on behalf of the local ministry to the Annual Conference Board.

So far, we have been applying a local church administrative model to the Wesley Foundation. More technical matters will arise when we discuss the *Discipline* directly. For now, let us apply the model to the other campus ministry programs of the Annual Conference Board.

Cooperative campus ministries follow the same model as Wesley Foundations. Wherever there is a Wesley Foundation board, policy and administrative duties fall to the Annual Conference Board as discussed above. Yet cooperative campus ministries contain some additional complexities. Usually another denomination is involved, and at least some of the decision making has been deferred either to it or to a joint committee. And, in many cases, such arrangements are desirable.

The guideline with cooperative agreements is this: all agreements must be approved by the Annual Conference Board, along with means of reporting on the uses of funds, property, and staff. In other words, the Wesley board must fulfill all of its responsibilities to the Annual Conference Board. That means that the other denominations must know, from the onset, that the Wesley board is an agent of the Annual Conference Board and must act within the guidelines and policies of the conference Board.

With ecumenical campus ministries we have to change our perspective on the model. Rather than seeing an administrative board relating to its Council on Ministries, we need to see one administrative board relating to another. In ecumenical work, one administrative group contracts or covenants with another to administer some work for it. It is like one congregation contracting with another.

The model here needs adjustment as well. In ecumenical campus ministry arrangements, the Annual Conference Board will have some of its own members on the other "administrative board," the ecumenical board. The Discipline requires a representative from the Annual Conference Board on the board of each local campus ministry it supports. [par. 732.4c(2)] In addition, the Annual Conference Board should have membership on any state or regional ecumenical campus ministry commission it works with.

In ecumenical work, the Annual Conference Board will negotiate with the other partners from other denominations. It will need to guarantee that the goals and aspirations of the annual conference are well represented in the program of the ministry. It will also have to make certain that it gets the kinds of information it needs, both to evaluate the ministry and to adequately present it to the annual conference.

The Board will also want to make certain that matters of legal liability have been adequately handled—property insurance, personal and corporate liability, coverage for the staff—and gain some clarity as to the ultimate legal liability of the supporting denominations.

The Board will want to guarantee the participation of the partners financially and for designated lengths of time. Each should bear its share of the weight, and no one should drop support without 12 months' notice, for example. In this category, the Board will also plan for annual or biennial reviews of the contract or covenant to assure its currency and to flag needed changes.

In ecumenical ministries, the Annual Conference Board releases some control. It receives in return the infused creativity of other partners. But it does not release its own responsibility to do all it can to generate effectiveness in that ministry. It is not an absentee landlord; it is a copartner in ministry.

When it works with local churches, the Annual Conference Board becomes, again, much like an Administrative Board. It, in essence, allows a local church to become its Council on Ministries. This may be for programs initiated by the local church and taken to the Board for funding or for programs begun by the Annual Conference Board.

In either case, the Annual Conference Board will view the activity as part of the annual conference program. It will set the guidelines and policies governing the flow of funds and the reporting and evaluating of the program. It also will determine the full pattern of accountability.

If the local church program involves funding staff for campus ministry, the Board will need to be clear about how that staff time is reported, and how it differs from staff duties that might otherwise be a normal part of the local church program. The point to remember is this: when Annual Conference Board funds become involved, so do the policies of that Board.

Of course, the Board may choose, as well, to have local church committees help carry out some administrative functions, just as it does with Wesley Foundations. Those decisions, which keep administration simple and helpful, work out best if there are written guidelines for local committees letting them know what the Annual Conference Board expects, and by when. For example, if the program simply involves a small grant to a local church, what kind of final report is needed and by when? If the program involves staff, the guidelines would include a designation of specific activities, an assessment of staff time to be invested, a statement of goals, and an evaluation process for measuring the effectiveness of the project.

In all of this, the cardinal point is that there are two kinds of functions: administrative and programmatic. In different arrangements those tasks are distributed differently. But in all cases, the responsibility for making certain that they are all cared for belongs to the Board. Those responsibilities are the Board's way of staying both on top of and ahead of the programs it manages.

The Discipline and the Annual Conference Mission in Campus Ministry

The *Book of Discipline* describes the Annual Conference Board's program in campus ministry at two levels. It has several paragraphs dealing with all campus ministry: Wesley Foundation or ecumenical. It has others that deal exclusively with Wesley Foundations. In this section of the Handbook we will deal with the paragraphs that pertain to all campus ministry supported by the annual conference.

To interpret and promote the United Methodist ministries in higher education which are supported by the general Church and those specifically related to the Annual Conference. [par. 732.4a(1)]

The Board plays a crucial role in interpreting and promoting campus ministries. It becomes increasingly difficult for campus ministries themselves to interpret their programs other than to a very few congregations. Meanwhile, the local churches' preoccupation with their own programs draws prior attention away from the campus. The result: an information gap. The Annual Conference Board, therefore, must devise ways to keep the ministry on campus before the people.

That kind of interpretation can be done routinely through conference newsletters and newspapers, and through inviting the campus ministries to provide leadership at pivotal events in the life of the districts and annual conference. For example, campus ministries could host district meetings, or provide worship leadership during Pastor's School.

Equally to the point is keeping those ministries on the minds of persons in the inner structure of the conference. We will discuss this more in a later chapter. But for now, focus on ways to keep the work and value of campus ministry before these four strategic groups: the bishop and cabinet, the conference Council on Ministries, the conference Council on Finance and Administration, and the Conference Council staff. Between them, they not only make significant decisions, they also create much of the attitudinal atmosphere of the conference. They need to be educated, informed, and inspired with the potential and program of the ministry on campus.

To recommend the policies guiding the Annual Conference in its program of ministry in higher education. [par. 732.4a(3)]

All major program policies belong to the annual conference. But the Annual Conference Board will be particularly careful to bring to the annual conference these policies about campus ministry: professional personnel, ecumenical covenants, salary and benefits, property and maintenance, and insurance and liability. The reason? These areas include something beyond program management. They include commitments the entire annual conference must honor.

For an example, consider ecumenical covenants and contracts. In this case, possibly three or four denominations have agreed to contribute shares for the salary and program of a campus ministry. If one decides precipitously to withdraw, it could leave salary, maintenance, or program costs dangerously underfunded. A policy, adopted by the annual conference, that it will always give its ecumenical partners one year's advance notice prior to any changes in support, provides both stability and integrity to the operation. Here the policy must belong to the entire annual conference. The conference, after all, yearly makes its decisions about budget—often based on waves of interest or troughs of worry near at hand. It can make alterations within any Board's program budget quickly, without adequate attention to the result. When the conference owns the policies and agreements, its actions take on another degree of seriousness and require much more deliberation. Policies taken to the conference should be of that character.

To provide counsel, guidance, and assistance to . . . campus ministries within the Annual Conference regarding their relationships to the state, and to interact with public higher education as it reflects on the wholeness of persons and the meaning of life. [par. 732.4a(4)]

This paragraph has two prongs, different but equally important. First, we will consider relationships to the state. On one level, this simply refers to the legalities of any not-for-profit corporation. Is the campus ministry properly chartered and incorporated? Are its legal documents in order? Does the facility satisfy local and state codes?

On another level, this has to do with safeguarding the campus ministry's rights and status. In some states campus ministries and other not-for-profit corporations have found themselves facing property tax assessments. Sometimes the target is the primary building, sometimes it is the parsonage. The basis for the assessment usually is in local or state regulations regarding tax exemption. The Annual Conference Board will need to be watchful and to seek the advice of the conference's legal advisor should such a case rise.

The second prong of this paragraph has to do with interaction with the state as it reflects "on the wholeness of persons and the meaning of life." Of course, the conspicuous thing about the state is that it seldom does such things, at least explicitly. But most state policies on higher education are, in fact, judgments about what is meaningful and what matters in making persons whole.

Campus ministries are among the most active forces on campuses on those very issues. In schools devoted increasingly to job training, they raise questions about the quality of life. In schools focused on manufacturing and marketing, they raise questions about environment. In schools carving careers in finance, they raise questions about justice and equity.

As campus ministries expose issues like these, they need the counsel and support of the Annual Conference Board. Persons in the pew, who view campus ministry as an advanced form of youth group, need the Board's interpretation of the significance of this form of ministry.

More to the point, however, are some of their activities which bring the campus ministries into conflict with the state. This may occur when the ministries make peaceful protests against policies of the university, or when they witness against military or nuclear sites. These events express matters of deep conscience. They sometimes also violate the law. The Annual Conference Board should have advance knowledge of these events and should apprise the campus ministries of their legal position. These are complex matters. But they are best dealt with openly and beforehand.

To oversee the management of the Annual Conference program of campus ministry in Wesley Foundations, local churches, and ecumenical campus ministries. [par. 732.4a(6)]

The Annual Conference Board not only manages its own program, it gives oversight to those who manage the local programs on behalf of the conference. As the discussion of the management model illustrated, many decisions about campus ministry must lodge with those doing the ministry. Releasing to them the authority they need gives them power and flexibility to do their mission.

But those ministries must accord with rules of good management. They must agree with the policies of the annual conference. Thus the expectation that the Annual Conference Board will oversee that work. The word *oversee* has its roots in the word for episcopacy: *epi* "over," and *scopos* "to see." As the episcopal leadership in the church demonstrates, this is an active function: to oversee is not the same as to overlook.

Among the items to be overseen: budget and finance, evaluation of staff and program, management of property, scope of mission.

In Wesley Foundations oversight can occur quite directly. It may also in programs funded by the conference but occurring in local churches. In ecumenical ministries it will have to be negotiated with the ecumenical partners and built into the contracts or covenants.

To identify and work with . . . campus ministries on issues of public policy that bear on higher education, especially issues bearing on access, equity, academic freedom, peace, and justice. [par. 732.4a(8)]

Campus ministries and colleges are not the only agents in the church's program on public policy. Public policy will gets its own chapter later. For now, notice that the Board has a mission in concert with campus ministry. Gathering, as it may, information from several campuses, the Board stands in an ideal place to help the church and campus ministries develop joint strategies on public issues.

Not only campuses, but states determine policies that affect higher education. States heavily influence tuition and fees. They have the capacity to enforce equal opportunity regulations. They can foster peace colleges and institutes on public campuses. And they can encourage, through scholarships and grants, the creation of programs in the public interest.

Together with its campus ministries, the Board can sponsor workshops on public policy. It can also join forces with other higher education associations to inform educators and college administrators of the interests of the church and its constituents.

Perhaps closest to the core of its concern for access is the Board's awareness that governments determine, in large part, who can attend college. With the resources of campus ministry, it can systematically bring that information to local churches and to the Annual Conference Council on Ministries. Then concerted and informed action can occur to protect the avenues that lead citizens to higher learning.

To present to the Council on Ministries and then to the Council on Finance and Administration of the Annual Conference the financial needs for adequate support of the . . . Wesley Foundations, and other campus ministries related to the Annual Conference for allocations of apportionments to the churches within the conference. [par. 732.4a(10)]

Most program boards of the annual conference present their budgets only to the Council on Ministries. The case is different for the Board of Higher Education and Campus Ministry. It presents its budget to both the Council on Ministries and the Council on Finance and Administration. Why?

The answer lies in the dual nature of campus ministry. It is a program. But it also has staff and property commitments. That suggests that the programmatic ingredients of the campus ministry budget belong with the Council of Ministries budget. But salaries and property costs, which are administrative and not programmatic, belong in a different category.

Two lines of thought guide this—one pragmatic, the other a matter of principle. Pragmatically, the problem lies with muddying budget categories. When all items in campus ministry are considered as program, it clouds the picture and gives no clear sense of which funds actually underwrite which activity. That leaves the Conference Council on Ministries with a vast and undefined lump of expenditures simply labeled "campus ministry." Lack of specificity makes it easier to cut budgets indiscriminately.

The matter of principle has to do with protection of the welfare of staff and protection of property investments. Both care of persons and protection against liability claims make it imperative that conferences see their responsibilities through. When all of the campus ministry budget is subsumed under the Council on Ministries program budget, and then conference program budgets are cut, the result in campus ministry is not simply the loss of a workshop or two. It means unpaid salaries or deferring needed maintenance of buildings. As a matter of principle, the Annual Conference Board must bring the conference to a responsible position on these matters. One way of doing that is to separate salary and property items from program items, bringing them directly to the Council on Finance and Administration and guaranteeing their support.

Another factor in the paragraph has to do with assessment of needs. That assessment ought to be a part of the routine operation of the Board. A budget calendar ought to be in place by which each campus ministry presents to the Board its preliminary and final budget and program statements. Those should be weighed against the entire program sponsored by the Board. Of course, the local campus ministries must be consulted at every stage.

Finally, the paragraph calls for the support of campus ministry to be by apportionment to the local churches. Conferences may expect campus ministries to raise some of their own funds. They may also seek to make campus ministry a special "mission offering" of the conference. None of that should mask the essential issue: campus ministry is a program of the annual conference and should derive its primary support from it. The system of apportionments should guarantee the basic necessities of the ministry.

To promote use of the United Methodist Loan Fund and to designate appropriate persons to represent the United Methodist Loan Fund on campuses, such persons normally being Wesley Foundation Directors or ecumenical campus ministers supported by the Annual Conference. [par. 732.4a(14)]

More will be said about the Loan Fund in a later chapter. Wherever there is a United Methodist supported campus ministry, the campus minister becomes the loan officer for the fund. The Board will probably have to apprise both the new campus ministers and their local boards of that. Loan forms are obtained from the Office of Loans and Scholarships in Nashville, Tennessee.

On campuses that have no campus ministries, an area pastor may be designated. That information should go to the rest of the conference so persons will know whom to contact. Students may also seek scholarships through their own local pastors, in the event there is no campus ministry.

To apprise . . . campus ministries related to the Annual Conference with regard to their charters and constitutions, reversionary clauses, and liability. [par. 732.4a(17)]

The Annual Conference Board ought to have copies of the charters and constitutions of each campus ministry it supports on file, along with all amendments. They ought to be reviewed by legal counsel prior to completion and upon amendment. In addition, those documents ought to be examined to be certain they accord with policies of the conference and of the Annual Conference Board. And, of course, their agreement with the laws of the state must be ascertained.

All church properties must have a reversionary clause. Chapter seven of the *Book of Discipline* speaks directly to the matter. All properties of the church are held in trust and, when they no longer serve their present mission, revert to the church. The charters are expected to reflect this.

In the case of ecumenical campus ministries, the covenants and contracts ought to clearly spell out the manner and degree of United Methodist ownership of the assets. They ought also to declare the disposition of assets in the event the ministry changes or dissolves.

To counsel United Methodist institutions about property and endowments entrusted to the institutions and to maintain and enforce trust and reversionary clauses in accordance with the provisions of the Division of Higher Education under paragraph 1516.3c. [par. 732.4a(18)]

Reversionary clauses have been discussed above. Paragraph 1516.3c refers to cases in which campus ministries do one of three things: 1) discontinue operation; 2) move to sever or modify their relationship with the church; or 3) violate terms adopted by the Board or the terms of grants of new capital or endowment funds made by any agency of The United Methodist Church. In those cases, the Board must contact the Division of Higher Education of the General Board of Higher Education and Ministry. The Division then carries out its required duties to protect the assets of the church.

To monitor fiduciary and legal relationships with United Methodist campus ministries and to assist Annual Conferences in their responsibilities in these matters. [par. 732.4a(19)]

This paragraph sets its view on the legal and financial relationships between the annual conference and its campus ministries. Those include many of the matters already discussed: trust and reversionary clauses, incorporation, rules and policies of the annual conference, proper budget control, and routine systems for reporting. Those reporting systems should move relevant data from the campus ministry to the Annual Conference Board and from the Board to the designated offices of the annual conference.

The Board should add to its agenda yearly audits of all financial reports and biennial surveys of property and liability insurance coverage. Along with the insurance surveys should go property examinations and audits. The latter will help keep a current account of all needed building maintenance and of the state and date of acquisition of all equipment. In addition to providing a responsible pattern of property care, those practices will aid in long-term budgeting for both property and equipment.

To evaluate . . . campus ministries related to the Annual Conference with concern for the quality of their performance, the integrity of their mission, and their response to the mission goals of the general Church and Annual Conference. [par. 732.4a(20)]

A special section will be devoted to evaluation later in this chapter. For now, notice four things about this paragraph.

First, the Board evaluates all campus ministries related to the annual conference. Ecumenical campus ministries, Wesley Foundations, and local churches (if supported by the annual conference) fall under this rule. In ecumenical settings the Board will negotiate with its partners for a process that meets the needs of all participating denominations. With others, evaluation will serve as one of its standard procedures of management.

Second, the evaluation is of the "ministries" and not simply of the campus ministers. The effectiveness of the ministry lies, in part, with the efficiency of the campus ministry board. Evaluation tests the strength of the local board. It also tests the adequacy of the local board's evaluation of its campus minister.

Third, evaluation also tests loyalty to a stated mission. That implies that each campus ministry has prepared a mission statement that has achieved the agreement of the Annual Conference Board. How else does one know whether a ministry has integrity? Evaluation is not arbitrary. It examines progress toward agreed-upon goals heading toward the fulfillment of an agreed-upon mission. That is what "the integrity of their mission" means.

Fourth, mission statements do not stand in isolation. They reflect the concerns of the larger church. Therefore, the missional goals of the annual conference ought to feed into those of the campus ministries. In ecumenical settings, all partners ought to bring denominational emphases into the process. When, for example, denominations set goals for increasing ethnic minority leadership, the campus ministries of the church ought to make their special contribution.

To provide resources for local churches and districts with programs of ministry to students or to campuses, and, where those programs receive financial support from or are designated as ministries on behalf of the Annual Conference, to ensure that the policies, standards, and goals of the Annual Conference Board of Higher Education and Campus Ministry are observed. [par. 732.4a(24)]

We will deal with this paragraph again in a later chapter. In the light of this chapter, however, notice the role played by the "policies, standards, and goals" of the Annual Conference Board. All campus ministry done by the conference lies under the supervision of that Board. And its policies must be observed. Local churches may have their own campus ministries, operating under their own sway. But when those ministries receive support from the conference or have been designated as conference programs, they represent more than the local church. They represent the conference. As such, they must observe conference guidelines. They must aim for conference missional goals. They must follow conference procedures. The same holds for districts.

The Annual Conference Board may have several devices for assuring this. It might allot money to churches and districts as grants, in response to grant proposals. The grant guidelines would include agreements about accountability, focus, and reporting. Or the Board may work with a local church Work Area on Higher Education and Campus Ministry, much as it might with a small Wesley Foundation Board. In that case, a designated liaison person might serve to keep Board policies visible.

To have available the names and addresses of all campus ministries supported by The United Methodist Church, and to supply the names and addresses of campus ministries supported by the Annual Conference to all districts and local churches. [par. 732.4c(1)]

Each year, the Campus Ministry Section of the Division of Higher Education publishes a directory of all campus ministries supported by the The United Methodist Church and its ecumenical partners. Copies are sent to chairs of Annual Conference Boards and to Conference Council offices free. When they arrive, the Board ought to place an announcement in the Conference newsletter encouraging pastors to use the directory to discover the names of campus ministers at the institutions their students attend.

The conference newsletter can also be used each year to introduce the churches to the campus ministries especially related to the annual conference. An additional mailing will help reinforce that introduction. A letter to each district superintendent could firm up lines of communication. New superintendents may not know the ecumenical campus ministers, especially those from other denominations.

In all cases, encourage pastors and local church Higher Education and Campus Ministry chairs to get and use that information early. Campus ministers can write to students prior to the start of the school year, if they get the names. Also, during the school year, if emergencies arise in students' families, campus ministers can be called to care for students' needs.

Of course, districts and local churches need those names for other reasons. Campus ministries can offer special programs to local churches. Districts planning rallies, will find campus ministers able to help them locate good leadership. Councils on Youth and Young Adult Ministries could discover important affinities with campus ministry staffs and students. Sharing names and addresses builds pathways between several of the important ministries of the church.

To ensure representation of the Annual Conference board on the boards of all campus ministries supported by the Annual Conference. [par. 732.4c(2)]

This strategy not only opens lines of communication, it strengthens ties between the Annual Conference Board and the campus ministries it supports. It helps answer the question "How can we stay close to the ministries, knowing and supporting them as we should?"

Boards may enact this paragraph in different ways. Some Boards have district representatives, and those representatives may also be assigned to the campus ministry board in their area. Others may ask each campus ministry to select one person to become a member of the Annual Conference Board. In some cases a person not on either board may be selected and given ex officio status on each. In a few instances, the chair of the local board becomes automatically a member of the Annual Conference Board.

This paragraph accomplishes two important tasks. First, it routinizes ongoing communication and fresh information flow both ways. That allows the Board to remain current on the ministry program and the ministry to remain current on the expectations of the Board. Second, it establishes the pattern of Board-to-board administration, which is what the *Discipline* requires. The local boards, not their campus ministers, are held responsible for the campus ministry. The paragraph helps set that firmly into an ongoing process of representation.

To interpret systematically to the districts, subdistricts, and local churches the conference program of campus ministry as a ministry to the whole campus (students, faculty, staff, and administration), encouraging their support, and urging United Methodist students of all ages to participate. [par. 732.4c(3)]

Three things stand out in the paragraph. The first ties to the phrase "interpret systematically." For most Boards, the task of managing the campus ministry program absorbs much time and energy. When the conference requirements for budget building and goal setting are added to that, scant time remains for advertising of any kind.

That is why the Board needs a system, a routine that automatically gets information out. The device can be simple. Perhaps a calendar designating a different campus ministry each month to place an article in the conference newspaper or to send its own newsletter to local churches. It may be a yearly Lenten emphasis, when students and staff from campus ministries go to local churches to lead worship or do seasonal programs.

That can expand to a pattern of mailings from the Board. The first year of the quadrennium, Guidelines for Higher Education and Campus Ministry can be sent to all local churches. The second year, send one of the papers about campus ministry developed by the Division of Higher Education. The third year, send a "yearbook" of campus ministries supported by the conference, showing photographs and containing articles about programs. The fourth year, send devotional materials for students developed by the Division of Higher Education. And, every year, help promote the prize-winning magazine for high school graduates and first-year college students, *Orientation*. The point is to build a system rather than to have to invent a program of interpretation each year.

The second thing that stands out is the phrase "ministry to the whole campus." In Methodist history, campus ministry began with the church "following her children to college." Campus ministry simply elongated local church youth ministry. The image of campus ministry in the minds of many people has become fixated at that youthful stage. But campus ministry has grown up.

Student work remains a staple of the campus ministry program. But campus ministers have long recognized an important truth: colleges are environments, and, to minister well one must attend to how the entire environment affects persons. That has led the ministry beyond maintaining and repairing persons, to working with the college to prevent personal breakage in the first place. Ministry with and to staff and administration becomes essential.

But the ministry reaches even further. Colleges are the intellectual and research "hothouses" of our culture. In them grow, in microcosm, the ethical questions—and attitudes—that shape our national life. Through campus ministry, the traditions and beliefs of the church enter the debate swirling about those questions. Students and faculty have the opportunity to measure the church's wisdom against the dilemmas of this day. In some cases, apart from campus ministers and Christian faculty, the voice of the church would be stilled in the very place that galvanizes lifelong attitudes.

The third thing to notice is the activity arising from the two words "encouraging" and "urging." We wish all United Methodists to support campus ministry and would like broad participation from all students. Those wishes expose the targets of the Board's activity: All churches support campus ministry; all students participate. To accomplish that, the Board should look beyond the activities of the campus ministry itself to the people in whose midst it is set.

It settles in the heart of the church. How can people in the pew undergird that program? What do they need to know? How can they—through the activities of the Board or of the pastor—see a direct connection between their beliefs and the ministry on campus? The Board ought to carefully develop a quadrennial plan, aiming toward a time when every United Methodist has the opportunity to directly support its program. And, of course, it ought to join with the entire conference Council on Ministries in its efforts to educate local churches about the missional significance of paying both apportionments and conference benevolences.

It also settles in the heart of the campus. At the least, the Board should underwrite programs that help campus ministers get early access to the names of United Methodist students on their campuses. Some conferences have achieved this by selecting one campus minister to receive lists of the names of college students sent from conference United Methodist churches. That minister then sorts through the lists and sends other campus ministers the names of United Methodists coming to their campuses. The Board can assist also by training local church chairs of Higher Education and Campus Ministry to get those names early (possibly by July 1 of each year) and by telling them to whom they should be sent. Giving them printed forms with addressed envelopes will help the process.

The Board can widen its circle or "urging" through its contacts with the conference Councils on Youth and Young Adult Ministries. It can also work with the Education Committee of the conference Board of Discipleship to discover ways to get campus ministry information into the Sunday School programs and the summer camps.

One cautionary note needs to be sounded here. Many Boards, having no system established for their own projects, fail to budget for them. Instead, the funds they receive flow through them to the colleges and campus ministries they support. The Board must build budgets that do both: support colleges and campus ministries and the Board's own projects.

To establish and review covenants and agreements for ecumenical campus ministry and to ensure that they are in harmony with the policies, standards, and goals of the Division of Higher Education of the General Board of Higher Education and Ministry and the Annual Conference Board of Higher Education and Campus Ministry. [par. 732.4c(9)]

Most ecumenical agreements predate the Annual Conference Board. The understandings that created them may have faded. The documents of their formation may have gone unread. The ministries continue in a momentum detached from their original inspiration. And, like long-ago launched satellites, they have been forgotten, as the church has turned its attention elsewhere.

Or almost forgotten. Upon occasion, those ministries flash into visibility—either when conference budgets are tight or when the ministries yank the church into places that discomfit the pew.

Ecumenical agreements need fresh appraisal. That is the task of the Annual Conference Board. The appraisal is not for the purpose of divesting from ecumenical agreements. It is for a fresh understanding of the covenant and programs of the ministry. It is also for the purpose of infusing the goals of The United Methodist Church and of the annual conference into the programs.

But the stakes go beyond that. Many denominations have begun a time of assessing their ecumenical commitments. Those assessments should not be done alone, but with the other ecumenical partners, to ascertain the continuing commitment of all. Those commitments should include a minimum time period for any partner to announce and enact changes. One good recommendation is this: all ecumenical covenants will be reviewed by all partners every two years; and no partner will change the terms of the agreement with less than one year's notice.

The Annual Conference Board, therefore, becomes the key player in the conference's ecumenical campus ministry agreement. And that holds also for the forging of new agreements. Wherever the inspiration for them arises—local church, Wesley Foundation, annual conference—the establishment of those covenants becomes the assignment of the Board. As it enters negotiations, it must know well the standards, policies, and goals of the conference. Those will determine its final judgment about an acceptable covenant. The Board will also let the ecumenical partners know, at the beginning, the expectations of United Methodists.

Special Responsibilities With Wesley Foundations

The duties discussed above refer to any and all campus ministries supported by the annual conference—Wesley Foundation, ecumenical, district, or local church. The *Discipline* gives additional direction for Wesley Foundations. Those ministries form a distinct denominational presence on college campuses. And they express the annual conference's ministry in a unique way. Hence, the additional guidance.

Each of the following segments of the *Discipline* locates a specific duty of the Annual Conference Board with and for Wesley Foundations. Their accumulative effect is to tie those ministries in closely with the life and mission of the annual conference.

To hold the Wesley Foundation Board of Directors responsible for the direction and administration of the foundation in accordance with the policies and objectives of the Annual Conference Board of Higher Education and Campus Ministry and the standards of the Division of Higher Education of the General Board of Higher Education and Ministry. [par. 732.4c(4)]

Several points stand out in this section. The *Discipline* here specifically forges this link between the Foundation and the Annual Conference Board: the Annual Conference Board holds the Wesley board, not the campus minister, responsible for operating the Foundation in accordance with policies of the annual conference and general church. Put squarely, the relationship is between Board and board. That means the Annual Conference Board must devise a way to guarantee that the Wesley board knows its policies, is trained to carry them out, and has a systematic way of reporting.

Further, the policy-setting responsibility of the Annual Conference Board is clearly established. That Board sets policies for the annual conference program with Wesley Foundations. There is no doubt about its authority to do so. But a caution is necessary. Those policies must be crafted to strengthen the Wesley ministry and to guarantee the conference the information it needs. Considerable latitude must be left to the Wesley board to craft a ministry sensitive to its best intelligence about its own campus. The purpose of the Wesley Foundation, after all, is not ultimately reportage, but ministry.

This section also implies that the Annual Conference Board will develop and retain a consistent line with its policies. Many Boards, because of changes in membership, become afflicted with forgetfulness. Not storing their policies and agreed-upon procedures in one place, not sharing them routinely with all new members and Wesley boards, not updating them for campus ministers—they grasp for makeshift ways to settle problems that have long had solutions. Better that the Board keep its policies and procedures in the forefront of its activities.

Finally, this section refers also to the "standards of the Division of Higher Education of the General Board of Higher Education and Ministry." What are those standards? They are not formal statements. There are no lists of standards and rules, apart from the *Book of Discipline*, that govern the denomination's work with Wesley Foundations. What there are, however, are accretions of learnings and informal advice that may have great pertinence to the practice of campus ministry. Those are made available through the publications of the Campus Ministry Section of the Division of Higher Education, through the training events that Section sponsors, and through consultation with its staff. All of those sources are highly recommended as the Annual Conference Board pieces together its policies and procedures.

To ensure that the Wesley Foundation Board is related functionally and cooperatively to the United Methodist local church or churches in the immediate vicinity of the college or university and the council of ministries or other organization of the district in which it is located. [par. 732.4c(5)]

The Wesley Foundation is the ministry of a connectional church. It is also a ministry of the annual conference. It needs to express that church connection more than programmatically; it must express it organizationally. And the church must also express its ties to the campus organizationally. The *Discipline* asks that both ends of that responsibility are cared for. And it calls on the Annual Conference Board to see that it is done.

The local churches and the district Council on Ministries closest to the Foundation need to have a place in their structure for the Foundation. That may mean a place on each Council on Ministries for a representative of the Foundation, and it may mean as well a place in the district and local church budget for the Foundation. It should also mean that, as the ministries of the districts and congregations take shape, the questions are asked often: "How might the resources of the ministry on campus enhance our programs? How might our program enhance the Foundation's ministry on campus?"

The Wesley Foundation board must also reflect its connectional environment. There should be representatives from the district Council on Ministries and from nearby local churches on the board. And they should function as liaison persons—making certain that news and needs flow both ways.

The Annual Conference Board can help make those connections. It can establish minimum requirements for the constitutions and bylaws for Foundations, indicating the number of members that must come from local churches and the district. The Board can, and possibly should, work directly with local church pastors and the district superintendent to explain this requirement of the *Discipline*, and to establish routine ways to fulfill it. Wesley boards and ministries occasionally undergo periods of flux. During those times, established procedures between the annual conference and the district and local church will provide the stability in structure needed by the Foundation. They will also assure consistent connectional support as a new ministry begins its way on the campus.

Finally, a word about those two words, functionally and cooperatively. Function comes from a Latin word that means "to perform." In the performance of its ministry, the Wesley Foundation relates to the district and local church. The nature of that performance will differ from one setting to another. But the performance is not a soliloquy. The second word secures the first: cooperation. There are two or more actors on the campus stage, and they are to act so far as possible in concert. That does not call the local church to do the Foundation's ministry, nor the Foundation the local church's. The Board, however, should actively draw each into a complementary role.

To determine whether or not the Wesley Foundation, when incorporated, may hold property and to ensure such property is held and administered according to the Book of Discipline of The United Methodist Church and the laws of the state in which the foundation is located. [par. 732.4c(6)]

This is likely to catch some Boards unaware. Most Wesley Foundations have existed longer than Annual Conference Boards, and acquired their own property long ago. They have assumed control of their property. In some other conferences the conference Board of Trustees has been assigned responsibility for all Foundation buildings. The situation, therefore, is not always straightforward. Nevertheless, this paragraph makes some things clear.

In the establishment of new Wesley Foundations, the Annual Conference Board makes the determination of whether or not the Foundation may hold property. That is not a decision of the Wesley board.

Further, even in the case of established Foundations, the Annual Conference Board determines whether the Wesley board can hold property. This refers both to the continued holding of presently held property and to new acquisitions. In some cases, for example, a Foundation may hold property in addition to its activities building. It may decide to sell that additional property and to retain the assets as an endowment. The Annual Conference Board will decide whether that can be done, or whether those funds must revert back to the conference or to the budget of the Annual Conference Board.

The *Discipline* also requires the Annual Conference Board to assure that the Wesley Foundation is incorporated according to the laws of the state in which it is located. In addition, it must be certain that the other requirements of the *Discipline* are met. For example, a reversionary clause must be written into the charter of the Foundation, guaranteeing that all properties will return to the annual conference if the Foundation closes or changes its denominational allegiance.

To determine the policies for nomination and election of Wesley Foundation Boards of Directors. [par. 732.4c(7)]

This paragraph reiterates the content of 732.4a(22), and the following comments apply to both.

Because Wesley Foundations are ministries of the annual conference, the annual conference elects their Boards of Directors. That normally occurs at the yearly meeting of the Conference. The Annual Conference Board makes the policies and procedures that assure that the names are in order and in place by the time the conference meets to elect.

What should those policies be? The nominating procedures of annual conferences differ markedly, and no single pattern will work for all. With that in mind, however, some general suggestions can be made.

First, setting policies for nomination and election does not mean actually doing the nominating. The Annual Conference Board determines how and by when. The Wesley board will determine, for the most part, who is nominated.

Second, the Annual Conference Board may require that certain categories of persons be elected. For example, it may require at least one local pastor, several faculty members, one or more students, specific representatives of district organizations (such as United Methodist Men, United Methodist Women, the district Council on Ministries, the Council on Young Adult Ministries). It may also require limits of tenure for board members.

Third, the Annual Conference Board should establish a calendar for Wesley boards, giving them a routine and schedule for their search for nominees.

Fourth, the Annual Conference Board should work with the annual conference Committee on Nominations to make its nomination and election process coincide with that of the conference. When do the names have to be made available for the conference nominating slate? Is there a conference tenure policy? Does the Conference have a pool of names that might be shared with Wesley boards?

Fifth, the Annual Conference Board should allow the Wesley board as much flexibility as possible. The local board knows the persons on and near campus. It also knows its own leadership needs. Its suggestions about nominees should receive great weight.

To determine, in consultation with local boards, the personnel needs of Wesley Foundations, to establish procedures for selection of professional staff, and to consult with the bishop and cabinet when securing the appointment of ministerial staff members. [par. 732.4c(8)]

Historically, Conferences have acquired Wesley Foundation professional staff in several ways. National searches, local negotiations, and routine annual conference appointments have been the most common. Each of these routines began prior to the time of the Annual Conference Board. Today, Boards are likely to find themselves in the midst of one of those already-established practices.

The 1988 *Book of Discipline* signals a change. It places the Annual Conference Board at the center of the hiring process for Wesley Foundation Directors. It is not autonomous, however. And it requires careful thought and skill.

In consultation with the local Wesley Board, the Annual Conference Board determines the personnel needs of the Foundation. The Annual Conference Board makes that final determination. It must, because it must not only know the needs of this one Foundation, it must balance them against the needs of other Foundations and against the resources available to fund ministries. But the best information available about the local Foundation comes from its own board. Its advice becomes a critical component in the final determination.

Once the determination of staff needs has been made, the Annual Conference Board establishes the procedures for the search for professional staff. It may decide, for instance, that the search may include diaconal and other lay persons. It may decide that a national search will be held, with all candidates screened by a joint committee of the Foundation and the Annual Conference Board, together with a member of the cabinet. It may decide to allow the Foundation to conduct its own search. However it is done, the responsibility for establishing the procedures belongs to the Annual Conference Board. It must ensure that the procedures work.

A very important consideration has to do with the Annual Conference Board's cooperation with the bishop and cabinet. First notice that, when securing the appointment of ministerial members, the Board must consult with the bishop and cabinet. Second, however, notice that it is the Annual Conference Board, not the Wesley board, that does the consulting. Put those two items together and you get this result: When episcopal appointment of a minister for Wesley Foundation is sought, the Annual Conference Board becomes the "pastor/parish committee" and must work through the bishop and cabinet.

A caution is necessary here. Bishops and cabinets take appointment-making seriously. Pre-established rules and habits guide their steps. For most, this new role for the Annual Conference Board will come as fresh and possibly surprising news. Boards will do best to begin talking early with the bishop and cabinet, prior to the time of appointment making, to build commonly agreed upon guidelines and procedures for seeking Wesley Foundation staff. The goal: a cooperative process that does two things: 1) obtains the best qualified professional staff for Foundations; 2) fits leadership on the campus to the needs and strategies for campus ministry adopted by the Annual Conference Board.

Special Issues in Campus Ministry

1. Campus Ministry Among Peoples of Color.
From 1980 until 1988, The United Methodist Church carried out a denomination-wide program to strengthen the ethnic minority local church. At its 1988 General Conference, the church moved that emphasis into the ongoing programs of every general board and agency. Now, each Annual Conference Board shares in that common, and uncommonly important, ministry.

The church's performance on campus among persons of color has been very limited. The number of Blacks, Hispanics, Native Americans, and Asians in campus ministry is very small. The same holds for the number of campus ministry units with successful programs with persons of color.

One reason for this is that more than half of all persons of color who attend college are enrolled at two-year community commuter colleges. Ministry at community colleges and among commuters poses its own problems—limited time on campus, large numbers of part-time students, no residential facilities.

But even where persons of color enroll on four-year campuses as full-time students, the church has seldom offered a ministry. Perhaps the exception is the campus of the historically Black church-related college. There, through its chaplaincy, the church has entered the lives of Black students in a rich variety of ways.

But that is the exception. Since 1980, the numbers of Native Americans, Hispanics, and Asians on American campuses has increased. The number of Blacks peaked in the early 1980s, dropped, and has now begun to rise. Add to that the increase in persons of color in the country's general population. California soon will be a "state of minorities," with no racial group comprising a majority of the population.

Campus ministry (at times with neighboring local congregations) may be the church's best chance of ministering with and to persons of color on non-United Methodist campuses. But the accounts in the church's bank of resources are shallow. Personnel are in short supply—there are few ethnic minority campus ministers, and few white campus ministers with the required understandings and skills. Money is in short supply—in many Conferences campus ministry budgets have been strained, and local units have had to raise substantial amounts for their own support. Experience is in short supply, as well—very few have built a base of experience broad enough to truly inform others about the ministry.

The Annual Conference Board faces a challenge of some proportion then. But it has allies, as well as good reason for activating ministry among persons of color. First of all, it has the congregations and ministers of Black, Hispanic, Asian, and Native American churches. It also has faculty persons with commitments to racial opportunity and equity. Consultations among those persons should provide a start.

Second, it has a cadre of well-intentioned but untrained white campus ministers. Having them work with the persons named above will open some doors. Also, bringing consultants in ethnic minority campus ministry to their campuses will give them specialized attention. The Campus Ministry Section of the Division of Higher Education can provide staff consultants. Also, the general church has begun to offer workshops to help white campus ministers learn how to do campus ministry with Blacks.

Third, the church has several caucuses of persons of color. Their names and addresses can be obtained from the Commission on Religion and Race. Among those groups a Board can find not only leaders, but resources for worship and study.

Finally, the Board must work with the bishop and cabinet to locate and train persons of color for ministry on campus. That may involve finding persons from other conferences. It may mean finding persons in congregations to do either full- or part-time lay ministry. It may mean identifying leadership among the young in local churches, encouraging them to consider the ministry, and supporting their efforts. Among that widening pool of persons, then, will come those to give consistency and continuity to the work on campus.

2. Evaluation.

Campus ministry is difficult to evaluate, moreso than many other activities of the church. Camps, for example, can be measured by the number of campers each year; local churches by membership growth. Determining per capita costs there comes down to dividing the amount of money spent by the number of persons participating. The results are quantifiable, comparable, and sometimes of more than casual interest.

Campus ministry, on the other hand, does not take in members. It does not register persons. It does not receive persons by transfer or by confession of faith. It is, by definition and *Discipline*, not a local church but a ministry "beyond the local church." A campus minister may have ten persons in counseling (occupying ten to fifteen hours each week), fifty persons in short-term or ongoing programs, and a hundred persons in programs he or she has referred them to. That minister may also speak to twelve classes of ten to forty persons, consult with or assist with a dozen student clubs and associations, and meet with ten or more members of the faculty and administration on matters affecting a thousand or more students. The minister may also be engaged with four or five campus-wide events that touch a thousand or more persons, and offer a benediction to a group of twenty-five thousand. Along with that, he or she may take programs to or make presentations at fifteen local churches with a combined membership of two thousand. Service projects may engage thirty people in villages of two hundred to restore homes of ten families. There is, in addition, the time it takes to get into a position to be able to do such things, and the actual planning that completes the preparations.

That illustrates the problem of using membership or attendance numbers to evaluate campus ministry. Even if one can derive some numbers, their meaning is not always clear or helpful.

One of the tasks before Annual Conference Boards is to develop an understanding of campus ministry. That understanding precedes any meaningful evaluation. The Campus Ministry Section of the Division of Higher Education has resources to help, resources that examine both the effectiveness and the faithfulness of campus ministry.

For now, Boards need to study and to proceed experimentally to develop evaluation tools. It may be best to begin by evaluating portions of the ministry rather than attempting a comprehensive scrutiny. The selection of the areas and the method ought to be done with the local board. And the focus ought to be upon agreed upon goals and programs. Each year the perimeter of investigation may expand. That will allow for testing, and for adequate time to assess the value of the learnings.

For example, the Annual Conference Board and the local board may agree to evaluate programs for nontraditional students and for faculty. That could be agreed upon at the onset of the school year. The campus ministry then would devise strategies for developing the program, establish a calendar, assign staff time and budget, and present a proposal to the Annual Conference Board. The two boards would then agree on reasonable outcomes for the first year. At the end of the year, the local board would do a complete analysis, comparing the outcomes of the program to the initial expectations, stating new learnings, and projecting next stages in the program. The Annual Conference Board would then respond, and together the two boards would build toward the next year. And, for that year, some new program areas might well be added. At all stages, both boards should have agreements about the time and nature of any reports and final reviews.

In that stage, and later as well, some Annual Conference Boards select teams to visit each campus ministry. Often an outside consultant is enlisted—one with useful experience in campus ministry. The team visits the campus, having made arrangements with the local board and the campus minister. With the help of the local board, they arrange interviews with faculty and staff from the college, students, other campus ministers, local churches—interviews intended to get as full a view of the ministry as possible. At the close of the day of interviews, the team visits with the local board and staff to feed back informally what has been learned. A formal report follows, both to local board and to the Annual Conference Board.

Whatever the evaluation procedure, one should be able to say three things about it:

- It is appropriate. It does not evaluate ministry using criteria drawn from different and dissimilar enterprises.
- It is ethical. It evaluates on the basis of clearly stated expectations and with the full knowledge of those being evaluated.
- It is educational. The point of the evaluation is to discover which programs accomplish the ministry desired by the local board and the Annual Conference Board. Further, it gives the Annual Conference Board all of the information it needs to interpret the ministry, to fund it, and to integrate it into the life of the conference.

3. Financing Campus Ministry.

We have dealt with this earlier in the chapter. There are, however, some other considerations. They have to do with campus ministry boards doing fund raising.

Most campus ministries raise a portion of their budgets. For some that portion is great, and much of the ministry is devoted to projects generating dollars. For others, the amount is small and can be raised in a short time through regularly scheduled activities. In any event, campus ministries that must raise funds face two challenges: to develop fund raising activities that also perform ministry and to produce enough money to keep the ministry strong.

Some campus ministers have become adept fund raisers, building ministries that both earn and serve. Some have even published books to help others learn how. The Campus Ministry Section of the Division of Higher Education also has resources.

But ultimately, the task of assessing how much the conference should provide and how much must be raised locally falls to the Annual Conference Board. As it prepares for that task, the Board should consider the following:

- Campus ministry is a mission of the annual conference, to be supported by apportionments to the local church. Although that apportionment may not satisfy the entire budget for the program on campus, it should satisfy a significant portion of it.
- The boards of directors of Wesley Foundations are nominated and elected by the Annual Conference Board. If local boards must raise money, the Annual Conference Board should locate and nominate persons with those skills.
- The Annual Conference Board can support its ministries by means other than apportionments—for example, by endowments, establishing higher education foundations, arranging for and promoting Advance Specials, and seeking funds through the annual conference Foundation.
- Campuses differ in their capacity to produce funds. Community colleges with a commuter student body seldom offer enough stability to organize persons to raise funds. Residential colleges offer large stable cadres of persons and better prospects for some kinds of money raising.

- Almost all campus ministers and their boards will require special skills if they must obtain significant parts of their budgets. New members and ministers will need special training immediately. Because they are engaged in a program of the annual conference, those persons ought to be trained by the Annual Conference Board.
- The Annual Conference Board should cooperate with local boards to locate potential donors and by planning to engage all of the congregations of the conference in supporting the ministry.

4. Student Movements.

Many states and jurisdictions have active student movements. In others, those movements are nascent and gaining momentum. On the national level, a formal organization of students is now in place. At every level, the Annual Conference Board has a role to play.

What are student movements? They are gatherings of college and university students, sponsored by Christian denominations, and involving students from several campuses. Usually they work through existing campus ministries and offer opportunities in addition to those available on the local campus. Their most common activities are regional or state-wide convocations or retreats.

Student movements involving United Methodists are not all of the same kind or structure. Some are ecumenical; some are solely United Methodist. Normally, United Methodists are strong supporters of ecumenical programs, and that holds for student movements as well. Even when the movements are "United Methodist" in name, they extend their welcome to persons from other denominations. Very often United Methodist annual conferences support both Wesley Foundations and ecumenical campus ministries, and their student movements blend both.

Some student movements are sponsored by Annual Conference Boards. Many have arisen through informal contact between campus ministers.

Student movements add enormous energy to campus ministry. They bring together persons from several campuses. They add the leadership resources of many ministries and universities. And they help students find a place in a church-related movement that transcends their own local campus. That final consideration provides for a subtle but significant shift in identity: on their own campuses it is their college identity that provides a common thread for bringing students together; in the student movement it is their Christian and United Methodist identity that provides the common thread.

Annual Conference Boards can encourage campus ministries to participate in student movements. They can provide incentives through goal setting and joint program planning. They can create budgetary support. They can assist by locating places for student movements to gather. And they can obtain and circulate resources from the Section on Campus Ministry of the General Board of Higher Education and Ministry.

Boards can also energize student movements by involving campus ministers and students in national events. The United Methodist Church has a Student Forum made up of students from each annual conference. The Forum trains student leaders, offers Bible study and worship, brings together persons from many nations, and plans for national United Methodist student events. Each Annual Conference Board is asked to send students to the Forum and to help with their expenses.

Once each quadrennium, United Methodists also sponsor a national student gathering. As indicated above, the members of the Forum are the planning committee for that event. Students from the world over attend the gathering, and Annual Conference Boards are asked to plan early to help large groups of students and campus ministers register.

The Annual Conference Board ought also to send campus ministers to national training events. Each summer two are held—one for new campus ministers and one for advanced training. At both events, student work is high on the agenda, and campus ministers can get information about student movements. Similar opportunities are provided at the yearly meetings of professional associations: the National Committee on Campus Ministry (NCCM) and the National Association of College and University Chaplains (NACUC).

Historically, student movements have produced significant leaders for the church. They have also helped to rouse the enthusiasm of local congregations for the work of campus ministry. And they give the Annual Conference Board a chance to play a direct role in placing students in life-changing contexts. The Annual Conference Board has an opportunity to help build those movements. Its campus ministries are the bricks; its attention, its plans, and budget are the mortar.

Conclusion

Through campus ministry the church reaches onto the non-United Methodist campus. Campus ministry has grown and changed over the years. While retaining its original ministry to students, it has enlarged to embrace the total campus environment. The Annual Conference Board, therefore, finds itself managing a much larger mission than many persons understand.

It also finds itself managing a quite diverse program, with Wesley Foundations, ecumenical campus ministries, and local churches all extending programs to the campus. To buttress those ministries, the Board keeps the annual conference and the local churches well informed.

None of that is done in a day. It grows, step-by-step, from one achievement to another. The Board, working in patience and planning for the growth of its work over four or five years, eventually gains the experience and understanding it needs to manage its mission and to receive, in return, the full joy of its contribution to the church.

Chapter Five

The Annual Conference Program In Higher Education Public Policy

Two themes have typified United Methodist public policy in higher education: access and choice. For nearly a century, private colleges were *the* educators of the American people. They appeared nearly everywhere, providing access to higher learning from urban centers to the remote frontier. They have continued to offer persons the choice of an education protected from many of the whims and foibles of political change.

From 1860 to the present day, however, both private and public education have undergone enormous change. One of the results of that change has been an awareness of the significance of public policy for all of higher education.

What is public policy? It is the accumulation of laws and regulations adopted by governments. Our interest in public policy is with the accumulation of laws and regulations that affect higher education. Those laws and regulations touch a great many lives and issues. They cover student aid, grants for special programs, civil rights laws, taxation, research, building codes, and much more.

Public policies are the instruments governments use to assure equality, opportunity, and safety. They are also the means used by governments to stimulate certain parts of the society or economy. Federal research grants to universities, for example, encourage study in areas that may strengthen defense or improve the country's competitive edge in international business.

Since World War II, the state and federal governments have become increasingly active in higher education. Today, they contribute more than $50 billion each year to that enterprise. Forty-six percent of all students get some form of financial aid—thirty-five percent from federal sources and fifteen percent from the state. That does not include financial grants given by both governments directly to colleges for buildings and research.

The church has supported the growth in government participation in higher education. It accords neatly with the church's own commitment to access for all eligible persons. That is one phase of the church's public policy activity.

Another phase has been the continued effort to protect choice in higher education. Government participation has meant more than student aid. It has meant a vast system of public colleges and universities. Those institutions receive the great bulk of government higher education money, particularly from the states. That channeling of public money has helped keep down the over-the-counter price of higher education to students—at least in public institutions. But it has also created a tuition gap between state colleges and those in the private sector.

To understand the problem of protecting choice, we need to clarify two important concepts: cost and price. Cost is the total amount of money it takes for a college to educate each student. Generally speaking, the cost per student is not much different in public or private colleges. Price, on the other hand, is what the student pays for an education. That does vary greatly. Why? The answer was hinted at above. Greater amounts of public money go into public colleges. Tax dollars help pay the college's bills, and therefore keep the price charged to students lower. Private colleges, on the other hand, get much less from the government, and therefore must charge a higher price to the student.

Obviously, if private colleges want to protect choice, they must discover ways to keep their prices low. They do this through several means: raising funds to use as scholarships and grants, increasing endowments to offset their operating costs, and keeping costs as low as possible.

But the private colleges have also protected choice through vigorous programs of public policy. They have supported state and federal programs of student aid. Through a series of Department of Education rulings, state and federal court decisions, and governmental legislative acts, it has been made clear that students who go to private colleges may receive government funds to do so. It has also been made clear that some kinds of direct aid to those colleges comports well with the goals and laws of the land. Those kinds of support give students a genuine choice in higher education.

The two broad themes of access and choice continue to resonate throughout United Methodist higher education. As the ranks of students have swelled (12.5 million in 1987) and the need for education has grown, so has its activity.

A fact of life for many now is this: decisions made in governments determine, in large part, who can go to college. The church's concern for access and choice now entail careful attention to what happens in the state and federal government. As laws are passed, the doors to education either open or close for significant portions of the American people.

United Methodists, with their historic commitment to higher education, have a stake in both of their historic themes. They believe in access, and therefore support programs that open the doors for all qualified persons. They believe in choice, and therefore support programs that keep private colleges and universities affordable.

To anchor that commitment, the church designated the Annual Conference Board of Higher Education and Campus Ministry to address public policy issues. The Board brings to the church needed facts about proposed legislation. It helps protect its own institutions. And it joins with others to weld together public policies that move this country closer to its vision of serving the public good through higher education.

The Makers of Public Policy

Who are the makers of public policy? We all are. At least through our votes and our efforts to influence our nation's leaders. But in a narrower sense, the makers of public policy are those officials, elected or appointed, who have been asked to manage our affairs of government.

The Annual Conference Board should know where basic higher education policies are set. Here are some locales.

Local governments set policies. Many of them have community college programs, supported through millage or other tax assessments. The decision to start a college, the choice of funding patterns, the fee structure, the array of curricular choices, and its connection with other colleges and universities will be decided locally.

State governments set policies. Most have legislative committees on higher education as well as state offices of higher education. In addition, some states have Boards of Regents that administer the state's institutions. Some states have also created systems of two-year colleges, often under a separate board. Other agencies also set rules that affect higher education: for example, tax committees and equal rights commissions.

The federal government sets policies. Both Houses of Congress have higher education subcommittees. The federal government also has a Department of Education whose head holds a cabinet level position. In addition, civil rights regulations, tax laws, and judicial decisions arising from other federal agencies may profoundly shape higher education.

Legislation and rules for higher education come from many sources in the federal government. While congressional higher education subcommittees and the department of education will propose a great many policies, others will do so as well. Decisions to limit charitable deductions from income taxes will affect philanthropy to colleges. Welfare legislation that requires recipients either to work or to attend school will determine, to a limited degree, who applies for college, and how it gets paid for. Defense legislation that budgets amounts of money for research will influence the direction of research (and the flow of funds) to certain universities.

Public policy in higher education is set in many places. As the Annual Conference Board becomes more sophisticated in this area, the connections will become clearer. And it will find itself more able both to alert the church and to make its own opinions known.

The Discipline and the Annual Conference Program in Higher Education Public Policy

We believe responsibility for education of the young rests with the family, the church, and the government. In our society this function can best be fulfilled through public policies which ensure access for all persons to free public elementary and secondary schools and to post-secondary schools of their choice. Persons in our society ought not be precluded by financial barriers from access to church-related and other independent institutions of higher education. We affirm the right of public and independent colleges and universities to exist, and we endorse public policies which ensure access and choice and which do not create unconstitutional entanglements between church and state. (par. 74.D)

This paragraph from the "Social Principles" lays both higher education themes plainly before the denomination. We believe in "access for all persons to . . . post-secondary institutions of their choice." Further, we believe that financial barriers ought not preclude the choice of a church-related or other independent higher education institution.

The paragraph also points directly at public policy. Providing higher education goes beyond the financial means of any church, in and of itself. But higher education also benefits more than the church. It lies in the public interest to support programs of education. Lack of education can be shown to link with poverty, crime, and other costly social problems. Education brings to most people their best chance to live self-sufficiently.

The church has a special, missional interest in access to independent higher education. United Methodists have 116 institutions of higher learning. They, together with other independent colleges, make an unparalleled contribution to the nation's welfare. While independent colleges enroll twenty percent of all college students, they graduate larger percentages than public colleges and send more students on to graduate and professional schools. They also have markedly better success with persons of color.

Because, in our society, social advancement usually rides on the back of educational advancement, access to independent education becomes supremely important, and especially to those who might be least able to afford it. United Methodists respond as citizens by asking their government to support access for all, and by safeguarding access to independent and church-related colleges. In them rides, for many, the best hope for graduation and social improvement.

The church does not make apologies for its belief that the public has an interest in the success of private, independent higher education. The state has a stake in ensuring the public good. Church-related colleges have played an obvious and successful role in that regard.

At the same time, the church preserves the line between itself and the state. It does not seek to flout the Constitution. Its colleges observe the laws that govern the use of federal and state funds.

That matter confuses many United Methodists. The Annual Conference Board may be called upon to clarify it. Students going to church-related colleges may receive federal and state aid. Church-related colleges may receive federal and state grants for buildings and for programs. But colleges may not use public funds for sectarian purposes.

The government has used three indicators to measure whether that line has been violated. 1) Does a denomination directly control the college (as opposed to its duly elected board of trustees)? 2) Is chapel (or some other religious observance) required of all students? 3) Are doctrinal or dogmatic courses in religion required of all students? Colleges may sponsor all manner of religious activities, so long as they honor these lines. Also, they must assure the government that government money will not be used for buildings that have sectarian purposes.

Avoiding unconstitutional entanglements, the church-related college can continue to offer its rich blend of values-oriented, quality liberal arts education. And the state has a stake in its doing so.

To interact with public higher education as it reflects on the wholeness of persons and the meaning of life. [par. 732.4a(4)]

This may seem lofty, and in two senses. First, that the Annual Conference Board may presume to work with those who govern public colleges and universities. Second, that the political forces shaping higher education meditate at all on the "wholeness of persons and the meaning of life." In fact, nearly every higher education decision either expresses an opinion about or has an effect upon the wholeness of persons and the meaning of life.

And those "meditations" take place at many levels. Many occur on campus, where daily decisions affect thousands of persons. Others are made in legislatures and governmental departments. Decisions about opening or closing campuses, strengthening or weakening programs, allocating funds for research (or instruction or sports)—all make implicit declarations about the meaning of the life the university intends to support.

The Annual Conference Board can approach public education in at least three ways. It can do so through its campus ministries—most of which are on public campuses. Campus ministries, working with students, faculty, and administration, have access to good information. Often, they will become active in issues that concern the campus. And, often, they will be the Board's most effective tool. The Annual Conference Board, therefore, should expect its campus ministries to act on matters like equal opportunity, civil rights, freedom of speech, students' rights, rights to privacy, dormitory conditions, and any of the other myriad concerns that affect the wholeness of persons.

The campus ministries should have time at Board meetings to acquaint Board members with the ways the colleges enhance and impinge upon persons. That way, state-wide trends can be registered. The Board will gain two positive advantages. It will be a better interpreter of the mission on campus. And it will know when issues are sufficiently general to warrant alerting the church and approaching state agencies.

A second way the Annual Conference Board approaches public policy is in its role as citizen. Members of the Board are citizens. The church is a corporate citizen of the state and the country. They have a citizen's title to help shape the program of the state. Proposed policies reported in the papers can become the grist for discussion and action by the Board. The Board ought to establish contact with higher education associations in the state—public and private. It can get on mailing lists, send members to meetings. And it can sponsor a yearly gathering of United Methodist state or federal legislators to discuss the future of higher education in the state.

A third way the Annual Conference Board "interacts with public higher education" is as a voice of the church. In a democracy, the church has no right to use the state to enforce its beliefs. But it is one group within a democracy, and has every right to enter the debate about the public good. Much of that debate has to do with higher education. The church does have opinions about quality of education, equal opportunity, basic rights, the purpose of public education. It has members who are students, faculty, and staff in public colleges. There is no reason it cannot speak from that base with legislators or with education officials. Indeed, there is every reason for it to do so.

To identify and work with the annual conference, church-related colleges, and campus ministries on issues of public policy that bear on higher education, especially issues bearing on access, equity, academic freedom, peace, and justice. [par. 32.4a(8)]

Intelligent and worthy public policy stems from a vision of the public good. The United Methodist Church has never blinded itself to its civic duty. Nor has it masked its desire to make a better society for all.

Education has, for the church, been one avenue toward that better society. But, until recent years, its approach to higher education public policy has been disparate and desultory. Now it has defined a center of gravity for its address to higher education: the Annual Conference Board.

While colleges, campus ministries, and occasionally annual conferences will individually deal with public policy, the Board is positioned to unite their efforts. That not only expands the range of debate, it pools vaster resources.

Although it has, as yet, scant public policy experience, the Board has the potential for locating common concerns. It has the strategic advantage of closeness to the conference Council on Ministries. It has proximity to those most immediately affected by higher education public policy. And it has the congregations of the conference to arouse and alert. It can speak to those congregations on behalf of the institutions. It can speak on behalf of the congregations and the institutions to public officials.

What is the Board's specific contribution to the debate about higher education public policy? The *Discipline* highlights five. It does not assume the Board has captured all of the world's expertise on them. But it does assume it has the desire to keep them before all persons on behalf of the church and for the public good.

1. Access.

We have discussed access in earlier paragraphs. Here we will discuss briefly the way, through public policy, access has been assured. The federal government, since the mid 1970s, has sought to guarantee higher education for all eligible persons. It does so through three kinds of programs: grants to students, guaranteed loans to students, and grants to colleges and universities. The state governments have complemented those programs by duplicating them and by opening public colleges and universities highly subsidized by government money.

As a result, every qualified student can have a college education. Access is possible. It may not mean access to the first college of choice. But it does mean access to some institution of higher learning.

However, the population of college hopefuls is putting strain on federal and state higher education budgets. Currently, 12.5 million persons attend college. Approximately 60 percent of all high school graduates attend college. Another 6 percent attend for-profit training schools. As the postsecondary pool of aspirants grows, the federal and state budgets become tighter and tighter. As a result, the funds available for grants spread farther, but grow thinner: more people become eligible for less money. Those grants are based on need. Obviously, the poorest will have first chance. One result has been that students who once might have received grants are driven earlier to use loans instead.

The problem affecting access is this: college costs rise, and the degree of student indebtedness of students increases. Other than for the very poor, then, the question soon becomes: how much debt can I assume in order to gain an education?

Related to this is another problem. It is retention, the other side of access. For example, among those schools to which access is easiest are two-year community colleges. Their prices remain very low. At the present time they enroll 50 percent of the Black, Hispanic, and Native American student population. However, those institutions tend to have the highest dropout rates among the colleges and universities. Often, they have large numbers of part-time teachers and overburdened offices of student affairs. Students who need assistance slip through the cracks. Our interest in access must transcend the problems of simple entry into institutions. It must lead to entry into institutions that heighten the students' chances for success.

2. Equity.

Equity has two faces. One looks within institutions; the other looks among them.

The United Methodist Church holds tightly to its commitment to equity for all persons within each institution, regardless of race, sex, or economic background. It raises questions about the opportunities for women faculty and administrators. It raises questions about the institution's seriousness in meeting the needs of persons of color.

The institution's performance in those areas is a matter of public record in most places. The Annual Conference Board should pay attention to reports that indicate the number of women and ethnic minorities in the employ of colleges. Incidents of racism on campuses ought to be responded to. College administrators need to know that the church cares about equity for staff and students.

A concern in recent times has been for Black athletes on predominantly white campuses. Studies have shown that football and basketball players have less time for class and study than other athletes or than students in general. Those two sports tend to recruit the highest number of Black athletes. Yet, in some major universities, the graduation rate of Black athletes is lower than 50 percent. Many now question whether those schools have a commitment to the success of those students as students. If not, and if sports performance is all that matters, equity has not been observed.

Among institutions the other face of equity is seen. Are all educational institutions treated equally? Are they allowed fair opportunities to educate? States provide equity when they offer students at private colleges grants to offset the higher tuition. The federal government supports equity when it holds all institutions to the same laws and policies.

But equity is not served when laws allow public institutions to sell more bonds to raise money to build buildings than private institutions may. Nor is equity served when public institutions not only have tax support, but they also raise funds among the traditional sources of support of the private sector. Nor is equity served when public community colleges are placed in the back yards of private colleges—especially in low-population regions. In these such cases, equity might suggest cooperation rather than competition between the state and the private college to assure affordable education to the citizenry.

3. Academic Freedom.

Academic freedom is one limb on the body of freedom of speech. It protects the right of enquiry, of speaking the truth as one has found it. In colleges, where learning advances through persistent inquiry, one expects new opinions and changing ideas. Some of them may not be popular. But popularity is not the point in academic inquiry.

Colleges sometimes feel public pressure to silence unpopular voices. To their credit, they seldom submit.

Yet, in ways new to academic life, freedom of speech encounters new dilemmas. For example, suppose a university receives a grant from the federal government to do research. Who owns the results of that research? If the college sponsors an international symposium, inviting some scholars from unfriendly nations, does the government have the right to silence the professors who plan to read papers based on research paid for by the government? Where does national security intersect with freedom of speech?

Major businesses also fund college research. Do they own the research done, in part, with their funds? Where does freedom of speech intersect with the expectations of private enterprise?

In church-related colleges a tangentially related issue may arise. Given the religious sponsorship of a college, does the church have right to silence a professor who speaks against its dogma? Where does the church's commitment to the unfettered quest for truth intersect with its belief in the truth of its doctrines?

Academic freedom is not only a political or constitutional matter. It is theological. If God is truth, can any discovery of truth be antithetical to the church? On the other hand, the church bases itself on certain beliefs about God—ought those to be preserved from inquiry and investigation? The Board will have the opportunity, perhaps, to think those questions through. When it does, it will tap one of the theological roots of higher learning.

4. Peace.

No greater challenge lies before the world today than quelling the hostilities among nations. Colleges educate nearly all who lead government and industry. Surely, if there is any garden for growing peace, the college is its soil.

Asking colleges about their commitment to peace drives right to the heart of their service to the public good. Yet, only a meager few have peace programs. Colleges continue to educate persons to do research about atomic energy without a corresponding effort to build a hedge of conscience about it. Career education gathers more and more students into programs that groom them for success but not for moral rectitude.

When it raises questions about peace, the Annual Conference Board does more than meddle. Its duty is to encourage its church-related colleges and its campus ministries to make peacemakers of mere students. In the local congregations it should sponsor debates about the effort of citizens to shape public policy in higher education, bending the will of the legislature toward education for peace.

That does not presume the Annual Conference Board knows more about peace than others in higher education. It only presumes that its bears peace on its conscience and that it knows the influence of colleges in shaping attitudes. In its conversations with other higher education associations, in its meetings with state legislators, in its conferences with regents and administrators, it raises the question: How does this college prepare persons to create a world of peace? The conversation goes on from there.

5. Justice.

If peace is the goal, justice is the means. Injustice casts the seeds of conflict. Justice shares the harvest of equity. The deep problems of injustice form a moat separating us from peace. They cannot be drained away; they must be crossed.

For students and for faculty, firsthand knowledge of injustice educates most quickly. College-sponsored work and study in places of poverty helps, in this country and in others. Serious debate about the effects of first world consumption on third world countries does so too.

64

Church-related colleges often provide excellent programs for students and faculty to experience and reflect upon the conditions for justice. Campus ministries have an excellent record of keeping the issue before colleges and the church.

The Annual Conference Board must understand and support those programs. Within the congregations, it becomes their advocate and interpreter. But it can do more. It can help bring persons from the campus to local churches to enlarge the arena for discussion.

Perhaps, more than the colleges or campus ministries, the Board can help the annual conference learn how peace hinges on justice, and how colleges are the door hanging on those hinges. Through the Council on Ministries it can report what it learns. Through the meeting of the annual conference it can advertise what it knows. Through district workers schools and mission schools, it can educate others about the importance of higher education in the quest for a just world. In the Board the resources of college and campus ministry collect. From the Board they flow to the church.

To apprise United Methodists of their historic commitment to and present mission in higher education. [par. 732.4a(9)]

This paragraph summarizes a portion of those above. Over the long haul, the Annual Conference Board will prepare itself to teach the church about a forgotten portion of its history: its mission in higher education. That mission received a high degree of the church's attention in the past. If the mission is to continue, United Methodists must recapture it.

Since the Civil War, the mission has included involvement with the government. At that time, the church, through its schools and colleges, carried out much of the federal program of educating freed slaves. Today, the church continues to serve the American people. It educates for values and for citizenship. And it continues work supported by the church and the government.

To learn that history is to see in bold relief the public face of the church. Without that, Methodism loses an essential ingredient of its identity. Although United Methodists have entered many arenas of social ministry, they have institutionalized their work in only a few cases: hospitals, homes, campus ministries, and schools and colleges. They are public witnesses to the church's mission. They stand on the cusp of the church and the world, uniting the finest interests of each.

The Annual Conference Board is the custodian of that tradition. It is also the teacher of the church. To restore that tradition is to win half the battle in revivifying the church's work in higher education public policy.

As part of its long-range plan, the Board could schedule the gradual release of historical and current information on this topic. It could also use the conference newsletter for occasional articles. Itinerating history faculty from church-related colleges to local congregations would personalize the story. Cooperative projects with the conference Board of Church and Society and the conference Board of Global Ministries could demonstrate how far-reaching the church's public mission is.

Programs in Public Policy

The task of building a management strategy for working with colleges and campus ministries will absorb the primary energy of most Boards for a while. Even so, however, the program in public policy can begin. Here are three ways to get that part of the program under way.

1. Connect with other higher education agencies in your state.

Begin with the United Methodist college in your conference. Indicate your interest in public policy issues. Ask which college officer deals with those issues, and get acquainted. Find out how to get information and resources. Tell that officer about the Board's Committee on Public Policy.

Discuss the Board's interest with United Methodist-supported campus ministries. Ask those ministries to keep the Board informed of public policy issues and of the strategies developed to respond to them. Arrange for campus ministers to attend national meetings where campus issues are discussed. Also ask campus ministers to share announcements with you about local and national convocations on public issues in higher education, such as racism, peace education, equality, and equity.

From any nearby college, get the names and addresses of all state higher education associations. The president or the library will be able to help you. There may be associations for public colleges, for private colleges, for two-year colleges, and for proprietary schools. Write to them, explain your interests, and ask to be on their mailing lists. Request the names of their members in your area. Invite local members to address the Annual Conference Board on public policy issues facing the state.

Contact the state board of higher education (it may have a different name in your state), and request its newsletter and announcements of any public hearings. Find out from that agency who is on the higher education committees of your state legislature. Write the chairs of those committees, indicating your desire to be apprised of new programs. Invite a member of the committee to meet with the Annual Conference Board. Or work with one of the United Methodist colleges to have a Congressional committee member speak on the campus.

Find out from the state associations the names of members of the federal legislature's higher education subcommittees. If any are from your state, write them to let them know you share their commitment to higher education. Again, request current information. Ask to be informed if hearings are going to be held in your area.

Finally, contact national associations of higher education and ask to be placed on their mailing lists, if possible. Among those you may contact are the American Council on Education, the National Association of Independent Colleges and Universities, the National Association of Land Grant Colleges, and the Council on Independent Colleges. Addresses are available in directories of associations in your library.

Also, subscribe to some higher education journals. Among the most useful are the *Chronicle of Higher Education* (a national higher education newspaper, published weekly) and *Change* (a monthly magazine). Again, your library will have addresses.

2. Focus on education and discussion.

As you move into public policy, focus first on programs that educate and stimulate discussion. Board members and others need first to become familiar with the issues.

Start with the Annual Conference Board. Bring reports from your public policy reading or from meetings of higher education associations. Invite members of higher education associations to speak to the Board. And devote a specified amount of time at each meeting to exposing the Board to its public policy environment.

Move next to the conference Council on Ministries. There, report at each meeting on the public policy issues discussed at the Board meeting. The report need not be long. The goal is to acquaint Council members with an area they know little about. If the Council has an annual retreat, ask to invite someone in higher education public policy to speak, or invite a professor from a church-related college who knows public policy to serve as devotional leader. When other program boards of the annual conference report on issues of public policy, identify your common interest with them.

Select specific congregations in which to hold discussions about higher education sometime within the quadrennium. Congregations near campuses may work best. Cooperate with the pastor and his or her council on ministries to do a program around the future of higher education, or the church's commitment to higher education. You may decide on a series of classes, or a one-day rally, or evening dinners with speakers. The leaders could be United Methodist legislators or college presidents, professors, or representatives from higher education associations.

As a variation, that congregation may choose to play host to other churches on the district. In that case, the district Council on Ministries could become an important ally.

Other educational opportunities are these. A yearly higher education breakfast for United Methodist state legislators and interested church members, with the focus on public policy in higher education. A debate on the campus of a church-related college, taking place near election time, and dealing with the state role in private higher education. A speaker at annual conference or at a district rally. A class on the church's educational mission at the district Christian Worker's School or the conference School of Missions, or a special section at the yearly Pastor's School.

On a broader plain, the Board could place occasional articles in the conference newspaper. In them, the Board must show clearly what effect public policies will have on persons. If some policies will deprive persons of access or choice, show how. If some will enhance equity or improve peace education, make it clear how and who will be affected. An occasional newsletter on "hot" issues will also serve to get ideas out.

At this stage, however, the Board may wish to stay somewhat shy of advocacy. It is learning, even as its helps others learn. But education must lead somewhere, and so must this. Eventually the Board will attempt another kind of activity: advocacy.

3. Become an advocate for church values and the public good.

The amount of time and money a church group can spend influencing public opinion is limited by law. Groups which are considered tax exempt by the Internal Revenue Service under Section 501c(3) risk losing their tax exempt status if they exceed those limits. The current interpretation of those limits can be gotten from the IRS. Under present law, however, 501c(3) organizations may seek directly to influence legislation and government policy.

As it matures in its understanding of public policy, the Board may move directly to make its values and desires known. It could do so as a Board, or by urging church members to write their legislators. Wherever possible the Board should work in concert with other associations.

Letters and petitions to policy makers are useful. They suggest quickly the breadth of support for a certain position. And church members have numerous opportunities to get signatures on petitions.

Board members should also make personal visits to policy makers. Those visits should be focused and the issue should be clear. It is best not to deal in generalities, but to have facts at hand. Appointments can be made through the offices of administrators and through the staff of legislators. At times, it is good also to schedule time with Congressional staff—the persons who actually research and write the preliminary drafts of legislation.

In some cases, the Board will gather persons most affected by a proposed piece of higher education policy. Day care legislation may affect single parents hoping to attend school. Tuition grant programs may affect persons planning to attend private colleges. Cuts in state support for public institutions may put greater pressure on private charities, or drive middle income students into greater debt to pay for their education. The Board can work with members of those groups to express its opinion about policies, and, in doing so, help those persons make their voices heard as well.

The Board needs to remember that most persons who will be affected by policies or legislation will not know about it until too late. In its public policy program, the Board acts as an early warning system. When it helps give voice to those who will be affected, it rescues the incentives of democracy. In so doing, its protects the public good.

Issues in Public Policy

The following eight areas include most of the public policy issues in higher education. Most will remain with us for some time to come. Two keys for sorting out the effect of these issues are these. They are two sides of the same basic idea. The more income available to a college, the better its program and the lower its price to students. The more money lost by a college, the more funds it must raise and the higher its tuition. Policies that support all of higher education do the most to ensure both access and choice.

1. Student Aid.
Most government aid to students is need-based. That means the government has a standard way of measuring the financial need of students, and that the most needy have priority.

Aid usually takes two forms: grants and loans. Grants are outright gifts, not requiring repayment. They normally go to the most needy students. Some states give grants that are not based on need to students attending private colleges, in order to equalize the difference in tuition between private and public colleges.

The government also subsidizes loans. Some are at lower interest than others, and some must be paid back sooner. Again need defines the issue: low interest loans with delayed paybacks go to those with greatest need.

Local banks make those loans. The government pays a service charge and pays the bank a fee so that the interest charge to students will be lower. The government also guarantees those loans and pays them off in the case of default.

Every budget year, state and federal governments debate the amount of money to be given in grants. They also debate how to distribute the grants—should full grants be given until the money runs out, should grants be smaller in order to give money to more people, should full grants become a right (an entitlement) no matter what the cost to government.

The government also debates loan programs. The amount of money in default on student loans in 1989 was $1.8 billion. How ought that problem be dealt with? Should colleges whose graduates do not pay back loans be penalized? Should loan programs be replaced by other approaches, perhaps by years of social or military service?

2. Institutional Grants.

Governments also give colleges grants for special purposes. Those grants have a twofold result. They strengthen some aspect of the college. And they keep tuition down, by allowing the college to use more of its own resources for student aid.

Research grants come from state and federal agencies. They sponsor study in areas of health, defense, science and technology, and in the arts. In the federal budget, for example, there are educational grants in the budgets of the Department of Defense, in the National Science Foundation, the Department of Agriculture, and in the National Institutes for Health. Those grants greatly enhance the quality of learning by attracting first-rate scholars and by keeping research moving forward.

Grants have also supported building and maintenance at colleges. In some cases, they have helped provide housing. In others, new facilities. Normally those grants go to institutions that serve special missions, but have severely limited finances.

Some programs target colleges serving special populations. For example, colleges that have high numbers of low income students qualify for grants to maintain their buildings and programs. Historically Black colleges receive grants to strengthen their programs and endowments.

All of those programs serve distinct social needs. But they live on a year-to-year basis, depending on the decisions of state and national legislators and administrators.

3. Taxation.

Most institutions of higher education are not-for-profit. Why should they worry about taxation? For several reasons. The Annual Conference Board should be aware of them.

First, many states and cities are taking a fresh look at property taxes. Charitable institutions used to be viewed as contributors to the public good. Now they are viewed by governments as revenue losses. In this time of budget constraint, governments have been asking how to recoup some of those losses. Colleges (and churches) have found some of their buildings assessed for taxation. Theaters and stadiums, parsonages and activities buildings have been challenged in recent years.

Second, colleges often have bookstores and snack bars. Those and other activities may compete with area businesses. But businesses must pay business income tax on what they sell. Should colleges also pay that tax; and if they do not, do they gain a competitive advantage over area merchants? Should the sale of essential college services then also be taxed; for example, should dormitories and cafeterias at colleges pay income tax, or are their services essential to the life of the institution, and therefore deserving of a special exemption?

Third, should endowment earnings be taxed. Colleges often underwrite their scholarship programs by investing major financial gifts. The earnings from those investments sustain scholarships. Businesses pay taxes on their earnings from investments. Should colleges as well? If endowment earnings are taxed, will the government then provide more scholarship money to students to make up for the college's lost revenue?

4. Income.

Colleges receive funds from many sources. Some laws make it easier, some more difficult, to raise income from those sources.

The federal government now allows taxpayers to deduct charitable gifts from their taxable income. But that deduction has been under scrutiny lately. Colleges, churches, hospitals, community services, and many other social institutions depend upon charitable giving to fund their work. What would be the effect on them if the charitable deduction were lowered or eliminated?

Persons give not only money, but property and other possessions. Those are currently tax deductible. But how ought their worth be evaluated? At their cost when purchased, or at their value when given? A painting purchased for $10,000 might well have attained the value of $100,000. If it is given to a college or a museum, should the donor be allowed a $10,000 or a $100,000 tax deduction? The willingness of major donors to give will certainly be influenced by taxation policy.

Colleges also derive income from selling bonds. Those bond sales allow colleges to build new facilities. Should all colleges, public or private, be allowed to sell as many bonds as they are able to, or need to? Or should private institutions have limits not applied to public institutions? Is there any reason in principle to apply different rules to one kind of educational institution than to another?

5. Civil Rights.

When institutions receive public funds, they must also adhere to federal civil rights laws. The recent Civil Rights Restoration Act underlined the extent of those laws. When colleges receive federal money for any program, the total program of the college must conform to the Civil Rights Code.

The Restoration Act also recognized that some colleges have religious commitments that affect their compliance. For example, denominations that do not believe in abortion are not required to offer abortions in their college-owned health services. But in general, colleges must observe the laws against discrimination on the basis of age, sex, religion, or race.

Those laws have generated many details in recent years. Are mandatory retirements still legal? Must part-time employees received the same benefit packages (especially maternity benefits) as full-time employees? Can colleges with strong beliefs about marriage and sex deprive unmarried female students of pregnancy coverage in their health care programs?

6. Proliferation of Colleges.

Although the number of traditional students has declined, some states have continued to build colleges. For the most part, they have been two-year community colleges. In many areas, they bring new and necessary services.

But at times they have been placed in areas that have small populations and an adequate supply of colleges. Usually those are private colleges. The addition of a two-year public institution puts strain on the resources of the private colleges and on the population. One question entering the debate is whether the state ought to cooperate with private education to enhance services to an area rather than to construct a competing institution.

Private campuses can be used for extension courses from state colleges; their faculty, staff, and management services can be contracted by the state; their facilities can be rented; their degree programs can be expanded. The public policy issue will be whether educational services can be expanded without undue increases in the number of institutions.

7. Welfare.

The federal welfare reform act offers welfare recipients new opportunities for education. But will that education be funded at a level that allows for genuine choice? Will it channel persons into short-term technical training, or will it allow for entry into full-term baccalaureate programs?

Further, will colleges receive supplementary grants for services that support welfare recipients? For example, for child care, educational and career counseling, remedial education, and weekend and evening instruction?

8. Proprietary Schools.

Proprietary schools are schools run for profit. Many have existed for years and have served an important need. Proprietary schools tend to serve high risk students, although they are not alone in that.

But recently questions have arisen about several of them. As a result of those questions, many educators are asking for reform of the proprietary sector.

That sector has the highest percentage of students receiving federal aid. Its students also have the highest default rate on federal student loans. The schools provide much less of their own money to fund student scholarships than do private not-for-profit colleges.

Some propriety schools have achieved notoriety as their practices have been made public. Chief among the problems has been the practice of recruiting students who lack the background to succeed at those schools. The schools have counseled those students to take out loans to fund their training. However, the schools lack good remedial systems, and the students discover too late that they can't handle the work or the schools can't deliver adequate services. The students drop out, colleges keep the money, the students keep the debt.

While those scandals do not characterize all of proprietary education, they have focused attention on the system of for-profit schools. And they have raised questions about accreditation and supervision—even more so now, in the light of the enormous drain on the federal educational budget caused by student loan defaults.

Conclusion

The Annual Conference Board has a valuable mission in public policy. To most, it will be new. The Board will need to work slowly and deliberately in this area, gradually building its program and its degree of expertise.

Fortunately, it has allies. Church-related colleges, campus ministries, the annual conference, state associations, United Methodist legislators and public administrators, and others—all form part of the connection. The Board should begin early tapping into that network. Then, through connection, education, and association, it can help its program grow.

Chapter Six

The Connectional Mission With The Annual Conference, District, And Local Church

The immediate pressures upon the Annual Conference Board will come from its colleges and campus ministry programs. Its long-term effectiveness may derive from its work with the annual conference, districts, and local churches. They are to the mission in higher education what irrigation is to farming—not the final product, but essential to give it dependability.

Most of the Board's programs require strong budgetary support. That support comes, finally, from the good will of church members and administrators. And that good will comes from a shared vision. Where does the vision come from? From inspiration and information. We have known about inspiration for years. What today's mission in the connectional church calls for is the other side of that equation: information.

More than ever, effective mission rides the currents of good information. Boards that care for good, systematic information flow, solve two problems (as well as they can be solved): they get the right information to the right people at the right time; and they prepare the soil for the seeds they must plant in the minds and hearts of the church's people.

For those reasons, the sights of this chapter will set upon information—not exclusively, but for the most part. Another reason for this has to do with recent history. When the Methodist Church and the Evangelical United Brethren Church united, they did not place a mandatory Board in the annual conference to care for Higher Education and Campus Ministry. The *Discipline* did allow for optional higher education committees or commissions, but annual conference response to those options was spotty, at best. For eight years, from 1972-80, other boards and agencies in the conference got well underway. They helped educate the church about the new structure together. They established styles of work together. Higher education was not among them.

Then, in 1980, the General Conference first mandated the Annual Conference Board of Higher Education and Campus Ministry. Since its inception, that Board has played a catch-up game. It has needed to make up for nearly eight years lost from educating the church; and it has had to do that while managing its program with colleges, campus ministry, and public policy.

The church still has much to learn about higher education. In this chapter we will consider some ways to inform the church, and some of the strategic maneuvers involved.

Our first concern will be the annual conference itself. Following that, we will outline a four-year plan for working with districts and local churches.

One additional word of preparation. The cumulative task of educating and making a functional connectional structure looks overwhelming. It is, if everything had to be done at once. Happily, that is not the case. Start where you are. Project a plan that extends over four to six years. Then, go at it step by step. Good education, like good farming, takes patience—and persistence.

Working With the Annual Conference

Like the moon, the annual conference has several phases. We are interested in two: the infrastructure for the conference's ongoing work, and the yearly meeting of the annual conference. Each of these needs to be addressed differently. Each needs to be informed, but about different things and in a different way.

1. The Infrastructure of the Conference.

Infrastructure is a word borrowed from the military lexicon and means the permanent installations forming the base for military operations. The term has been transported into other organizations as a handy way to label those more or less permanent groups whose work form the basis of their program. The prefix *infra* (meaning "below") indicates that much of what those groups do may not be visible to everyone all of the time, but is below the surface. Nonetheless, they strongly impact the quality and direction of corporate life.

The groups forming the infrastructure need accurate information. They need it in a timely fashion. Generally, they must make significant decisions, based on secondhand knowledge. They receive reports. They also prepare reports, suggest budgets, assign personnel, determine meeting places and agendas, decide upon training and informational events, and make long-range plans. Obviously, what they know (or don't know) matters a good deal. The efficient Annual Conference Board will make certain those groups are well informed.

Which are those groups? They are the following. Consider them as pools where essential information collects, is blended, ordered, and then released in strategic amounts.

- the Cabinet
- the Conference Council on Ministries
- the Conference Council Staff
- the Conference Council of Finance and Administration
- the Conference Trustees
- the Conference Committee on Nominations
- the Conference Program Committee
- the Conference Committee on Emerging Ministries
- the Conference Long-Range Planning Committee

We'll look at each of these briefly. But first, one general principle. The Annual Conference Board or its Executive Committee ought to consider how to create routine communication

74

with each of those conference groups. That consideration ought to involve four questions: What information does this group need in order to help us carry out our ministry? By when is that information needed? How does it get there? How can we get timely feedback from those groups so that our work can be done effectively?

The Cabinet. Each Annual Conference Board ought to have a cabinet representative. This will create a solid basis for arranging campus ministry appointments as required by par. 732.4c(8) of the 1988 *Book of Discipline.* It will give the cabinet access to all conversations concerning changes in campus ministry personnel, and will create the basis for the necessary consultation. It will also help alert the Board to cabinet discussions bearing on campus ministers.

The bishop and cabinet, of course, have other interests in higher education. Many bishops sit as members of a college's board of trustees. Although the bishop may not always be able to attend Conference Board meetings, a cabinet representative could bring the bishop's report. In some conferences, district superintendents also serve as school or college trustees. One of them could serve as cabinet representative, securely tying together three parts of the higher education program: college, cabinet, and Board.

Boards must recognize the general value of keeping the bishop and cabinet informed about the activities and goals of the Board. That helps the bishop and cabinet in their interpretive task. Also, it ensures them against surprises—often unwelcome features in the lives of senior administrators.

The Conference Council on Ministries. The chair of the Annual Conference Board is a full member of the conference Council on Ministries. Campus ministers, college representatives, and committee heads all must make certain the chair has accurate information prior to those meetings. News from those groups, good or bad, ought not come to the chair from third parties.

The task of the chair at those meetings is partly representational and partly educational. For most Council members, ministry in higher education will be remote and obscure, compared with other programs of the council. The chair must represent the missional strength and bent of the program. That means knowing facts and figures and reporting them.

Because Councils have concentrated so long on matters closer to the local church, the Board chair will have to help them extend their grasp of their mission. That means education. One way to do that is to continue to ask the Council to consider the higher education dimensions of its work. In almost every program of the Council, something might be added through the resources of campus ministries and church-related colleges.

Through campus ministers and church-related colleges, the CCOM might find worship leadership, demographers, business instructors, bookkeeping consultants, career guides, computer consultants, lecturers in religion and other topics, dramatic groups, guidance on political issues, educational and teaching guidance, continuing education, fund-raising ideas, and much more. What is there that a conference does that does not have a higher education dimension? The chair must help get higher education and its resources into the missional lexicon of the conference. The CCOM offers a prime opportunity.

The Conference Council Staff. Because of their versatility, conference Council staff members often become the threads that weave through the entire conference. Often, they meet with the cabinet, the Council on Ministries, the Council on Finance and

Administration, the Trustees, conference planning and strategy committees, Camping Commissions, and district Councils on Ministries, to name but a few. They frequently have the task of preparing reports, drawing up agendas, channeling information, and of helping chairpersons determine the processes for meetings. They are invaluable.

The Board should have a liaison person from the conference Council staff. That staff person (or, if there is no liaison, the conference Council Director) needs to know the Board's program well. Reports and phone calls should be made routinely. Arrange for consultation prior to Conference Board meetings and Council on Ministry meetings. Discuss budgetary needs and strategies. The conference staff is especially helpful with promotion. Getting the right information into those hands helps get it into the hands of others.

The Conference Council on Finance and Administration. Into this pool runs all of the information about conference budget and conference income. Finance and Administration does not usually make program decisions, but its decisions do affect program.

The Annual Conference Board, contrary to other program boards, has access to Finance and Administration, as indicated in par. 732.4a(10). The reason for that has to do with the Board's commitments to salary, property, and institutional support, in addition to program. Normally, the Board's program budget should be submitted with the Council on Ministries budget.

CCOM and CCFA members are not accustomed to this procedure. And, in some conferences, it may not be politic to insist upon it. However, getting information about its special needs to the right places smooths the ground for the Board's work. When key people appreciate the salary, property, and institutional commitments of the Board, they weigh their decisions about the conference budget differently.

Finance and Administration, for example, is the setting for discussing separate and guaranteed budget line items for campus ministry salaries (perhaps as a part of the conference administrative budget) so that salaries don't suffer when program budgets are precipitously cut. It is also the place to consult to secure funding for building and maintenance, so that conference owned campus ministry buildings do not fall into dangerous disrepair. Here, also, support for colleges can be built into the institutional support budget.

Both CCOM and CCFA, then, will need information. The Board will need to get its own goals for financing its program clear. Then, through consultation with the chair of Finance and Administration, it will take the steps needed to lay a basis in fact and precedent. Here, too, it comes down to representation and education.

The Conference Board of Trustees. There is no single pattern across the church for ownership of conference properties. In some conferences, all properties—camps, campus ministries, conference centers—are owned and under the management of the conference Board of Trustees. In others, the Trustees hold title, but the actual management is done by program groups; for example, the Annual Conference Board handles insurance and maintenance of Wesley Foundation buildings. In others, Wesley Foundations fall completely under the aegis of the Annual Conference Board.

In the first case, the Board must create a liaison to make certain that the Trustees have adequate information about the properties. A yearly reporting system ought to inform the Trustees about routine maintenance, deferred maintenance, and planned alterations.

Insurance ought to be reviewed yearly with the Trustees. And procedures for unscheduled maintenance and major expenses ought to be developed. A liaison person between the Trustees and the property committee of the Annual Conference Board could ease information flow both ways.

In the second case, the Trustees are the nominal holders of the property, but all costs accrue to the Annual Conference Board. Still, information flow is needed. Through the Trustees, for example, insurance might be made available on a group basis that could save the campus ministries money.

In the third case, the Board will still want to retain contact with the Trustees. Special funds or policies of the conference may be vested with the Trustees. The Board will need to know about them.

No matter what the relationship with Trustees, the Board and the Trustees have one very important item in common: the legal documents of the conference. All conference charters, titles, and other property documents should be kept in one place and be reviewed at least once a quadrennium. That information may prove critical in times of sale, disputes over ownership and use, or litigation.

The Conference Nominating Committee. Three tasks require communication with the Nominating Committee: Wesley Foundation Boards of Directors, college trustees, and Annual Conference Board members.

The *Discipline* requires the Board to set the policies for the nomination and election of Wesley Foundation Board members. [par.732.4c(7)] Those nominations must coordinate with conference nominations. And, as in most conferences the annual conference does the electing, there will be a conference schedule for getting the names on the slate. There may also be conference policies applying to all Boards. Good, early information, will keep the process synchronized.

The Board has special responsibility for trustees of church-related colleges when the conference nominates, elects, or confirms those trustees. [par. 732.4b(3)] That responsibility is discussed in chapter three. The process requires consultation with the Nominating Committee.

Many annual conferences elect Board members by the quadrennium. While replacements and changes are handled year-to-year, the year preceding the quadrennium usually sees the major work done. Not many persons have had higher education experience, and that usually means that conference Nominating Committees know little about the precise talents needed by the Annual Conference Board. The Board, therefore, needs to keep the Committee informed.

Two kinds of information should go to the Committee routinely. The first, information about kinds of special expertise needed by the Board. This could include persons with college teaching and administrating experience, persons with budget and fund-raising skills, persons with backgrounds in political science, persons with legal training, persons with advanced degrees, persons representing certain districts, and so on.

Second, information about specific persons you would like on the Board. Do not be afraid to name names and to inquire about interest. When you discover persons who can strengthen the ministry in higher education, write down their names and addresses. Get them into the nominating pool early.

The Conference Program Committee. This Committee usually determines the floor schedule for the annual conference. It also allots space for displays and exhibits.

The Board will have to compete with others for time on the conference schedule. But early communication of its hopes and plans will give the Board a better break with the schedule.

The Board has things to offer the conference, as well. As the Program Committee plans for worship and special evenings, the Board can use its contacts with campus ministries and colleges to locate leadership: speakers, music, drama, media presentations, and more. Working with the Committee, the Board can demonstrate ways higher education can add dimensions to many activities.

The use of space at annual conference gets less attention than it deserves. With the Program Committee, the Board can locate special regions for presentations and displays. We will discuss this further in the next section.

The Conference Committee on Emerging Ministries. Not all conferences have these. But many do have some place where the new needs and ministries of the conference get their first hearing. The Annual Conference Board has contributions to make here on two scores. First, it has inroads into colleges and can find experts to help in the analysis of new ministry proposals. Site development, demographics, institutional management, and other expert advice will help focus discussions of emerging ministries.

Second, the Annual Conference Board has emerging ministries of its own. Community colleges now provide Boards with some of their greatest challenges. With 50 percent of all Hispanics, Blacks, and Native Americans who are in college enrolled in those institutions, the church has a special need to center attention there. New welfare legislation may send thousands of the poor back to school. That suggests new ministries of deeply significant kinds. In those and other areas, the Annual Conference Board offers the church one of its best chances to be in ministry on the moving edge of the future.

The Conference Long-Range Planning Committee. Not all conferences have this committee either. But several have begun to turn their attention to the shape of the conference for the years ahead. If Emerging Ministries lay out the contexts of need, planning committees suggest structures to respond to them.

With the increased concentration on the local congregation among United Methodists, both needs analyses and suggested structures tend to reflect local church based options. There are others. In fact, institutions now shape the majority of human life. The church that neglects its ministry to and through institutions only gets to deal with people during recess.

Higher Education and Campus Ministry may be one of the few conference Boards that does the bulk of its work through institutions. The importance of that ministry must not be lost on the church. One voice that must be heard in long-range planning, then, is the voice of higher education.

2. The Annual Meeting of the Conference.

Like presidential elections, annual conferences are great educational opportunities. Those opportunities often remain orphaned, abandoned to find their own ways through rules of order and a rat-a-tat of hurriedly given reports. Narrowing the focus of conference to reports has kept from the eyes of many the full ambience of annual conference. Were that seen, the whole conference might become a lively classroom.

As the Annual Conference Board prepares itself for the annual meeting, it ought to keep in mind the various settings available at conference. Then it can prepare itself for each kind of occasion the conference offers.

First, the formal presentation. Usually, through presenting legislation or by bringing a yearly report, the Board has an opportunity to address the entire conference. The Board, of course, orchestrates the presentations of the colleges and campus ministries. They must be considered as one piece and tightly drawn together. If college presidents or campus ministers also address the conference, they should be carefully coordinated by the Board and come as part of the Board's moment in the spotlight. The conference Program Committee must be alerted to this early in its preparations.

The formal presentation ought to deal with matters that demand a public hearing. Don't report on or discuss what might as well be printed and passed out. Nor should numbers form the basis of the report—they are difficult to remember and tend to blur in tired minds—unless some crucial action at hand builds on those numbers. If it does, use placards, projectors, or some other visual device to get the numbers before the eyes of conference and keep them there.

Try to use floor time to convey the spirit of the mission in higher education. Tell about people affected by the programs. Describe achievements that teach about your fondest goals for the ministry. Set sights on ways the campus and the world are better because of your program.

If a critical issue needs discussion, make certain your presentation illustrates the human issues at stake. If there are questions from the floor, answer them briefly and honestly. Try to deal with them from within the Board, rather than calling on presidents or campus ministers; you must demonstrate the competency of the Board and its management. Plan the presentation carefully. Practice it, and remain within time limits.

As important as the moments on the floor are, the days in the environment of conference may matter more. In many ways, the more vital question for the Board will be: how can we use the entire environment of annual conference to teach about our ministry in higher education? That question reveals some favorable possibilities.

Annual conference meets where there are walls, doors, floors, ceilings, rooms, entry ways, exits, lounges, cafeterias, yards, walkways. It occurs in the midst of group business, worship, coffee breaks, dinners, casual conversations, and plain milling around. How might each of those places, each of those times transform itself into a moment of learning about the ministry in higher education?

Some examples might suggest the way. Every wall, and especially those over drinking fountains, are places for posters—posters from every United Methodist school and college, posters showing campus ministry pictures, posters advertising the Black College Fund or United Methodist loans and scholarships. Entry ways are places for handing out pins or ribbons with higher education messages or slogans on them. The area used for coffee breaks might have an entire wall of pictures from student projects at the campus ministries supported by the annual conference.

Ushers can come from campus ministries and colleges, wearing special identification badges. Worship leadership could be furnished from United Methodist faculty. Packets can await persons in their rooms and be filled with colorful brochures about the higher education programs their conference dollars support. Singing or drama groups from the colleges and campus ministries can provide entertainment during coffee breaks or out of doors between sessions.

During the report, graduates of church-related colleges and campus ministries and recipients of United Methodist loans or scholarships can be asked to stand, then be given a colored ribbon with a pin saying: Ask me how the church helps students.

Begin having a higher education dinner at conference. Coordinate it with the colleges and seminaries that have special dinners there. For one conference, unite forces with the colleges and seminaries, bring in a major speaker or entertainment, and issue special invitations to conference leaders to join you.

During election year, invite a United Methodist legislator (or legislators) to visit conference for a banquet and a speech on the church, the state, and higher education.

These are a few ideas. Your Board will think of many more, as soon as it turns its mind to the entire ambience of the conference. And, as it does, remember the resources of the general church. Special emphases like the Africa University bring fresh attention to the higher education mission. Lina H. McCord itinerants from the Black College Fund bring a lively message about an historic ministry. Resources telling about college and campus ministry can be had in quantity. And videotapes are available for display rooms and higher education events.

The Board can enliven conference for itself and for others. Through the brightness of its presence, it brings the excitement (and the theology) of the church's work. And as it does, it educates the people called United Methodists.

Working With the Local Churches

The Annual Conference Board of Higher Education and Campus Ministry has many tasks to perform. Fortunately, there are several other members of the higher education team. As the Board works with them and helps train them, its programs will expand and become more effective. Those members are:

- the local church chairperson for Higher Education and Campus Ministry
- the district chairperson for Higher Education and Campus Ministry

This section explains some strategies for training those members of the higher education team. Because that training proceeds gradually and requires consistent attention, some Boards will form a "Connectional Relations Committee" to look after it. Whether or not your Board forms a special committee, you may want to assign someone to manage this part of the program.

Strong ties to the districts and local churches will reinforce the Board. The more people who share in the ministry in higher education, the better the atmosphere for positive votes on the floor of annual conference, for ongoing ministries to students, and for affordable church-related colleges.

We will consider first the work with local churches. This section does not complete that topic, however. Much more will be said about local churches in the section on the work of the district.

Many churches and charges have a chairperson for Higher Education and Campus Ministry. Most do not. One task of the Board is to help the chairs who are now in place to carry out worthwhile programs.

This section presents a plan that will allow the Board to assist local churches with their programs. It relies heavily on sharing resources and channeling information. That assistance should be sufficient for now and will let the Board concentrate its efforts on the district. As the district program grows, step-by-step, it will present more and wider options to the local church. And, as those options increase, so will the number of churches that elect a chairperson for Higher Education and Campus Ministry.

A. Identify the local church chairpersons for Higher Education and Campus Ministry. District superintendents keep lists of all local church officers. Their names and addresses can be gotten from the district office.

Contact the church-relations officers or chaplains of the United Methodist colleges nearby. Many have recruited alumni and friends in local churches or parents of United Methodist students and have trained them to represent the college. Most colleges will be pleased to cooperate in training their local church representatives to carry out programs of the annual conference as well.

Talk with the campus ministers supported by your annual conference. Many campus ministries have contacts, alumni, or representatives in local churches. Their lists will help you discover interested persons.

When you assemble your own list of contacts in the local church, separate those who are elected Higher Education and Campus Ministry chairs from those enlisted by colleges and campus ministers. Ask the pastors of the latter group to appoint them as members of the Higher Education and Campus Ministry Work Area in the local church.

B. Assemble a resource kit for the chairpersons and local church contacts. There are several resources for local church programs in higher education. A kit could be sent free to each chairperson including:

- a letter from the chairperson of the Annual Conference Board welcoming the local church chair to the team, identifying the appropriate member of the Board to contact for help, and telling about some future plans for programs and resources;
- a copy of *Guidelines—Higher Education and Campus Ministry* (available through the district or conference office or from Discipleship Resources);
- a copy of *College Bound*, a booklet describing all United Methodist schools, colleges, universities, and seminaries;
- a copy of *Orientation* magazine;
- a list of the campus ministries in your state and the surrounding states (obtainable from the *Campus Ministry Directory* sent free to your conference Council office yearly);
- a newsletter from each of the campus ministries and church-related colleges related to your annual conference;
- brochures from the Office of Loans and Scholarships and the Black College Fund (obtain from the Division of Higher Education);
- information about the Special Days offerings that support higher education: World Communion Sunday and United Methodist Student Day;
- an information sheet to be filled out by the local church persons describing programs in higher education they have carried out during the past year;
  —a form for reporting to you the amount of the Student Day offering;
  —forms for sending campus ministers and chaplains the names of students from the church who are or will be attending college on their campuses;

—forms to send the names of high school juniors and seniors to church-related colleges.

C. Cooperate with those who are doing training for local church leaders. Several colleges have begun training the local church representatives. Usually they bring the representatives to campus, tour the facilities, describe their program, give them a college resource kit, and introduce them to staff members available to the local church. If the college related to your conference has a training event for local church representatives, ask if the Board can join in the project. You might meet with the college officials ahead of time to coordinate efforts.

Many districts have yearly Christian Workers' Schools. Those schools offer classes for three or four nights to lay people holding offices in local churches. If your annual conference has such schools, ask your conference Council Director how to arrange for a class for higher education chairs. If one can be worked out, invite campus ministers and United Methodist college staff to help with plans and leadership.

Developing District Leadership
For Higher Education and Campus Ministry

Your program will work best if you have a district chairperson for Higher Education and Campus Ministry. Those persons may represent the Conference Board on the boards of directors of United Methodist supported campus ministries on their districts. They may also represent the Board on the district Council on Ministries—indeed, they should do so. But their primary assignment is to patiently develop a program linking local churches in their districts to campus ministry, church-related colleges, and to the Annual Conference Board. To do that, they will need also to be full members of the Board.

A. Selecting the right person. Some districts elect a higher education chair who is automatically a member of the district Council on Ministries. In those that do not, it will be up to the Board, in consultation with the district superintendent, to select one. If there is no Council on Ministries, the Board will still gain many advantages by selecting a district representative.

Here are some things to consider as you select one:

- Many of the activities of the district chair will be carried out in the evening.
- The district higher education program builds by increments, one year's program leading to the next. Continuity matters!
- Some experience with campus ministry or church-related colleges is useful.
- An interest in students and in the young is essential.
- If the district has no Council on Ministries, seek a representative from another district organization—United Methodist Men, United Methodist Women, or cluster groups.

That list of considerations has led some Boards to select lay persons rather than clergy—principally because they tend to be available more in the evenings and because they are less apt to move.

As for one other consideration, knowledge of the job, there very likely will be no one who qualifies. The position is too new to have built up a reservoir of trained leaders. The Board will have to do the training, gradually increasing the experience and the responsibilities of the district chairpersons. The remainder of this chapter presumes that to be the case.

B. Preparing the district chair for the job. Most of the education for the district chairperson will be on-the-job training. But the Annual Conference Board can do two things immediately to prepare the chairs for the task.

First, hold an orientation session, preferably with all of the district chairs together. During the orientation, explain the four-year plan discussed in this chapter. List all assignments that fall to the chair—membership on campus ministry boards, membership on the district Council on Ministries, attendance at Annual Conference Board meetings. The budget available to each chair should be clearly presented, along with instructions for submitting expenses.

Second, a steady flow of resources should be arranged for each chair. Among them should be:

- all informational mailings from United Methodist colleges related to the annual conference (If there are none, select those from states nearby);
- all newsletters from campus ministries supported by the annual conference;
- the minutes of all Annual Conference Board meetings, whether or not the district chairs are members;
- copies of *New Perspectives;*
- mailings from the General Board of Higher Education and Ministry about Special Days, the Black College Fund, and the Hispanic, Asian, and Native American Fund (HANA).

The Work of the District Chair: A Four-Year Plan

Year One: Sensitizing the District

During their first year, district chairpersons learn about the church's higher education program. As they learn, they share. As they share, they make others sensitive to the role higher education could have in the life of the district.

To begin with, the district chair speaks for higher education in the district Council on Ministries. When programs are discussed, the chair asks the Council to think about ways the Wesley Foundations, ecumenical campus ministries, and church-related colleges might participate. What are the higher education dimensions of each project of the district?

The chair also reports to the Council. At each meeting of the Council, the chair should present information taken from the newsletters of the colleges, and campus ministries and general church. If some faculty have been honored, it should be reported. If some students have gained recognition, it should be reported. If a campus minister has taken students on a work project in an impoverished area, it should be reported. The goal is to establish the higher education consciousness of every Council member.

In the process, the district chairs will become more knowledgeable as well.

During the first year, some chairs might also begin to make phone contact with local churches, using the questions suggested in the plan for year two.

Year Two: Coordinating

In the second year, the district chairs add a second function to the first. They discover what the local churches are doing in higher education ministries, share that information among the churches, and encourage coordination of some programs.

The work of coordination begins with discovery. Each chair should be given a list of local church Higher Education and Campus Ministry chairpersons. Then, either by making phone calls or by sending questionnaires, they should learn about each church's program. Some useful questions are:

1. Did you celebrate United Methodist Student Sunday? If so, how? Did you take an offering for the Loan and Scholarship Fund? How much did you receive?
2. What have you done to recognize college administrators, faculty, or staff who are members of your congregation?
3. Do you have any members who are students? How many are away at college? How many are living at home? Are any of your other members taking classes? What do you do to keep in touch with students who are away at school? What do you do for those who live at home? What do you do for your "nontraditional" students?
4. Do any students from nearby colleges worship with you or participate in programs at your church? If so, what programs do you have for them?
5. Have you had representatives of a campus ministry or church-related college in your church this year? Who were the representatives? The president? Chaplain? Campus minister? A choir? Drama Group? Deputation team? What did they do? How did you care for them? For example, did your members help house choir members? Did a Sunday School class host the president, chaplain, or campus minister?

As the district chairs discover the programs already going on in local churches, they should share that information in three places: the Annual Conference Board, the district Council, and, most important, with other local churches.

When the chairs discover that two or more churches are carrying out similar programs, they should tell those churches, suggesting that they share ideas and cooperate in some of their efforts. For example, if two congregations traditionally host choirs or drama groups from campus ministries or colleges, they may try to coordinate their schedules, jointly provide housing for students or have a program together. Or, if two have college nights for seniors, bringing an admissions officer from a nearby church-related college, they might cooperate by sponsoring a program for the teens and families of both churches. An enlarged program would allow them to invite representatives from additional colleges and churches.

A once-a-year district higher education newsletter would help the chair coordinate programs. The newsletter could contain brief descriptions of programs carried out in local churches, including the names, addresses, and phone numbers of the persons responsible. Local church members will then be able to talk among themselves about higher education. When they do, they will discover many new ideas and much that they have in common.

Year Three: Programming

By their third year, the district chairs will be ready to initiate their own programs. At this point, too, their working arrangements may change. Task groups may form made up of members of local churches with whom the chairs hope to do projects. Districts may nominate and elect a higher education committee. Other district organizations, such as the Council on Youth Ministries or United Methodist Women, may select higher education representatives.

In order to manage this stage of their work, the chairs will need to establish contact with leaders of the church-related colleges and campus ministries in the annual conference. One of their prime objectives will be to bring those people or their representatives to the district or to local churches.

Here are five programs that could be initiated by the district chair. Ideas for many more will spring from conversations with churches, colleges, and campus ministries.

1. College Fairs. If five or more churches are interested, a college fair can be a fine event. A college fair brings teens and their parents together with representatives of colleges. The fairs include presentations on such topics as "How to Select a College," "Financing a College Education," "When to Apply to College," and "How to Prepare for College." The heart of the college fair, however, is the time parents and teens have to talk directly to admissions officers. Plenty of time should be allotted as well as adequate space for several conversations to take place at once.

To arrange for a college fair, contact the admissions offices of the United Methodist colleges that serve students from your annual conference. Enlist them for the program and for the planning. Then contact either the president of the district Council on Youth Ministries or the higher education chairs from several churches with youth programs. Arrange a meeting with them and the college representatives.

Begin advertising early, making certain that high school juniors and seniors and their families are invited. Arrange to use a church with a room large enough for the whole group to assemble and for several display tables from the colleges. Decide early what topics the college representatives will address. Admissions officers have a good sense of what students and families need to know. Most of them are also experienced with college fairs and will have valuable advice to give.

2. Higher Education Talent Pool. Local churches often need outside leadership. College ranks are filled with specialists. A talent pool is a project that brings them together. The talent pool is a list of the names of college professors and administrators, of campus ministers and students, who have talents needed by the church. The district chair initiates the search for talent and is the link between the college and the campus.

To start a talent pool, contact the campus ministers and the church-relations officers at colleges in the annual conference. With their help, develop a list of United Methodists and others at their institutions who would be willing to be speakers, consultants, or teachers for one-time or short-term events at local churches. The list should include the names of the persons who are willing to serve, their special topics (such as archaeology, computer programming, biblical studies, local history, office management, career planning, family management, etc.), what their expected remuneration is (travel expenses only, cost per day, or college covering all costs), and how to arrange for their visit. Print the list and mail it to all local churches.

If it is best for local churches to work directly with those in the talent pool, simply print a yearly list with the required information. Otherwise, the district chair may serve as the contact person for the churches. That has the advantage of allowing the chair to know who is coming and to coordinate the visit with other interested area churches. A list of available talent still needs to be circulated, along with instructions for contacting the chair.

While gathering data, it is good to find out whether choirs, drama groups, and deputation teams can be scheduled for the district. On occasion, in exchange for overnight housing, those groups will tour churches or perform at district-wide events. The chair can help plan the itineration, enlisting a task group from several churches.

3. Youth Group Programs. Many high school juniors and seniors have begun making plans for college. Several know by the late winter of their senior year which college they will attend. But not many know what to expect during their first few weeks on campus.

Campus ministers spend a good deal of time counseling first-year students. They are familiar with the predictable crises and confusions of freshman life. Spring, therefore, is a good time to bring campus ministers to youth groups or to take youth groups to campus ministry centers. Guided by the ministers and students from the campus ministry, they can discuss potential problems, learn about survival skills on campus, discover where to seek help, and anticipate some of the predicaments and temptations of their early days on campus.

Many students have never set foot on a college campus. The campus minister could take them on a tour, indicating the kinds of support services colleges offer and helping them understand the function of some of the college's offices. They will also see how the church extends its ministry to them on campus.

Campus ministers and chaplains have many skills for working with youth. The district chair should find several ways to connect them with the work of the district Council on Youth Ministries and should encourage local church Higher Education and Campus Ministry chairs to work closely with the counselors of their youth groups. The youth group program just described could be an excellent way to start working cooperatively.

4. Campus Days. As district chairs become more familiar with people who work on the campuses, they will discover that colleges are eager to welcome visitors. Given some advance notice, they will arrange tours, provide programs, and extend other amenities to guests.

Many groups in the district would enjoy a day on campus, a chance to learn more about the college or campus ministry. Among such groups are United Methodist Men, United Methodist Women, youth groups, parents and teens, clergy, and senior citizens.

The district chair can serve both the college and the churches by a) helping the college extend its invitation to groups in the church, and b) encouraging church groups to include the colleges in their plans.

5. Vocational Counseling. Most colleges have offices of Career and Life Planning. While their first duty is to the students on their campuses, they can, with sufficient notice, offer services to the church. If so, the district chair might work with them in ways that genuinely serve the church. Here are two.

Youth group members could be invited to take vocational interest tests, perhaps during their normal meeting times. Those tests would then be sent to the college for analysis. Later, the college would invite the students to campus for a day. During that time, a counselor would speak to them about career choices and educational preparation. They would receive the results of their tests and have time to talk with professors who know about their career areas. The day on campus could also provide time for a tour, for play, and, possibly, for hearing a concert or watching a game.

Another service the college may offer on a limited basis is counseling for persons who wish to change careers. While the demands for that kind of career counseling could exceed the time colleges can make available, they may wish to offer limited services. For example, a district Christian Workers School could have a class on "Making Career Transitions" taught by a member of the college staff. A class might be offered in a local church. Or a full-day convocation might be held on the campus.

In both projects, district chairs and their committees become the agents who bring the resources of the colleges and the interests of the church together.

Year Four: Strategizing

With three years of experience working with local churches and districts, the Board will know better the conference's needs for higher education programs. It will also know the needs of colleges and campus ministries that require access to the entire conference. The Board then must develop a strategy for working through all of the districts and with all of the local churches. Here are two examples.

1. Recruiting and training local church chairpersons for higher education and campus ministry. As the district program in Higher Education and Campus Ministry grows, it reaches more churches. If the district chairs have continued to sensitize, coordinate, and program, nearly every local church will have been phoned, written to, and invited to several events. The time is ripe for a conference-wide strategy to recruit and train local church chairpersons for Higher Education and Campus Ministry. Its success will depend heavily on cooperation among members of the entire higher education team—colleges, campus ministries, district chairs (or committees) and the Annual Conference Board.

The Board should organize a planning team, including all district chairs, representatives of campus ministries, and staff members from the colleges. Together, they should design a program that:

- brings the services of the colleges and campus ministries to the churches,
- shows the churches how to minister to students and faculty,
- shows the churches ways to support the work of the colleges and campus ministries,
- explains the programs of the general church (for example, the Black College Fund, HANA, Loans and Scholarships),
- offers ideas for organizing activities in the local church.

The team should also coordinate efforts to contact local churches, to recruit people for training, and to encourage pastors to select higher education chairs if they have not done so.

The training may be done in conjunction with a district Christian Workers School or at the facilities of a college or campus ministry. Wherever it is done, enhance its effectiveness with announcements, reports, and articles featured in the conference and district newsletters.

2. Meeting the needs of institutions. Colleges and campus ministries will turn to the Annual Conference Board when they have special needs. And the Board, as their chief representative in the annual conference, will need to work with them, creating a strategy for reaching the churches.

A campus ministry unit, for example, may have suffered severe property damage. If the budgets of the Board and the annual conference cannot underwrite its repair, other sources of funds will need to be found. The Board and its connectional team will develop a strategy for saturating each district with information about the need. A special Sunday offering may be requested, with district chairs and committees enlisting local churches, sending out information, and getting reports on the offering. The Board may back up the effort by getting pictures and articles in the conference paper. And, as with all projects of this sort, it will clear its plan and schedule with the annual conference and district Councils on Ministry.

As another example, colleges may wish to increase the number of scholarships they offer to United Methodist students. They and the Board may create a strategy to visit every local church within one year. Their goal: to encourage churches or individual members to establish scholarship funds for students who wish to attend church-related colleges. The Board, through its district teams, would arrange schedules for visits, coordinate them, do informational mailings, and find ways to highlight the contributions of the college to the church. Again, programs of this magnitude would be cleared with the district and annual conference Councils on Ministries.

Conclusion

The Annual Conference Board not only works with colleges and campus ministries, it reaches out to every local church. As its district workers gain experience, its program grows in effectiveness. And, as the annual conference builds upon the resources of higher education, its programs gain depth and scope.

Because the Board is new, those benefits remain to be shown. In the next few years, the Board will taste the pleasure of showing something new to the church. The process will include a lot of receiving and disseminating of information. It will, of necessity, mean doing many things for the first time.

A carefully laid plan, covering three or four years, will help the Board to move strategically and to measure its progress, and should do much to cure the absent-mindedness of the church about its role in higher education. As the districts, local churches, and annual conferences begin to comprehend the enterprise, the gifts of higher education, like the gifts of the three wise men, will mark the future of the church.

Chapter Seven

The Annual Conference Board
And The Programs Of The General Church

The Annual Conference Board of Higher Education and Campus Ministry is the connecting link between the annual conference and the general church. Through it, denomination-wide programs reach districts and local churches; and, through it, districts and local churches have access to the resources of the denomination.

The agency assigned to work with the Annual Conference Board is the General Board of Higher Education and Ministry. The GBHEM provides services and resources to the annual conferences through its Division of Higher Education. This chapter outlines the work of the Division and the services and resources it offers. It also describes the programs of the general church, showing ways the Division assists the Annual Conference Board in carrying them out. Finally, it reviews important administrative tasks that the Annual Conference Board fulfills on behalf of the general church.

Two Kinds of Work

The Annual Conference Board does two kinds of work on behalf of the general church: programmatic and administrative. The *Book of Discipline* describes the Board's programmatic role this way:

To interpret and promote the United Methodist ministries in higher education which are supported by the general church and those specifically related to the Annual Conference. [par. 732.4a(1)]

To provide the connectional relationship between the Division of Higher Education of the General Board of Higher Education and Ministry and the Conference, districts, and local churches. [par. 732.4a(2)]

The Board's administrative tasks are much narrower:

To counsel institutions about property and endowments entrusted to the institutions and to maintain and enforce trust and reversionary clauses in accordance with the provisions of the Division of Higher Education under Par. 1516.3c. [par. 732.4a(18)]

To confer at once with representatives of the General Board of Higher Education and Ministry to determine what resources and aid the Board may be able to provide and to enable the Division of Higher Education to carry out its responsibilities in the event that any educational institution, Wesley Foundation, or other campus ministry moves to sever or modify its connection with the Church or violate the rules adopted by the division in accordance with Par. 1516.3. [par. 732.4a(21)]

Several activities fall within those two kinds of work. The *Discipline* describes some. We will suggest others. A look at the organization and work of the Division of Higher Education—the Annual Conference Board's chief resource in the general church—will set the stage.

The Division of Higher Education

The Division of Higher Education is organized to assist the Annual Conference Board in carrying out its tasks. Each of its sections and offices provides resources and services created specifically for annual conferences and local churches. Knowing those offices and sections will help the Board find the means it needs to do its work.

The Division of Higher Education has two major sections and two offices. The sections are: Campus Ministry and Schools, Colleges, and Universities. In addition to them are the Office of the Black College Fund and the Office of Annual Conference Relations and Public Policy Programs. Each section and office has three general responsibilities:

- to represent its area of responsibility to United Methodist, ecumenical, and other agencies;
- to work directly with its constituents (campus ministries; schools, colleges, and universities; historically Black colleges; Annual Conference Boards);
- to provide resources and services to the Annual Conference Board of Higher Education and Campus Ministry.

The Division also works closely with the Office of Loans and Scholarships.

The *Discipline* gives the Division a further responsibility: to work with the University Senate to determine which schools and colleges may be approved for listing as United Methodist institutions. The associate general secretary of the Division serves as executive secretary of the Senate, and Division staff serve as liaison between the schools and colleges and the Senate. Because the Senate is discussed in the chapter on schools, colleges, and universities, only a synopsis of its duties will be listed here. For a full description, see the *Book of Discipline* (pars. 1517-1521).

Approval by the Senate is required before any school, college, university, or theological school may call itself a United Methodist institution. Approval is also required before institutions may receive funds from annual conferences, General Conference, general boards, or other agencies of The United Methodist Church.

To obtain approval, an institution must demonstrate satisfactory performance in four areas: church relatedness, financial stability, academic program, and institutional integrity.

To assure itself that the institutions are performing satisfactorily, the Senate insists that each one be approved by its regional academic accreditation association. In addition, the Senate assigns a team to read each institution's accreditation reports and other documents, and to visit it for on-site interviews with the trustees and president, the faculty and staff, and with students. During the visit, pastors of area churches are interviewed, along with the bishop, a district superintendent, and the chair of the Annual Conference Board of Higher Education and Campus Ministry.

The Senate also:

- represents the common interests of United Methodist educational institutions;
- encourages the development of programs in United Methodist educational institutions that address and reflect the values held in common by the church and the institutions;
- maintains, in addition to its campus visits (which normally occur once each ten years), a system for an annual review of the viability and program integrity of the institutions;
- determines which colleges, universities, and theological schools qualify for the training of United Methodist clergy.

Special Days and Programs for Higher Education

To work with the annual conference Council on Ministries and with districts and local churches to interpret and promote higher education ministries supported by special days and funds: Black College Fund; Hispanic, Asian, and Native Americans Educational Ministries (HANA); United Methodist Student Day; World Communion Sunday; and other funds and special days related to higher education ordered by General Conference or Annual Conference. [par. 732.4a(13)]

General Conference has linked the efforts of the local church, the annual conference, and the General Board of Higher Education and Ministry in four important programs:

- the United Methodist Student Loan Fund and the United Methodist Scholarship Program, both supported by the United Methodist Student Day offering.
- the Black College Fund, supported by an apportionment determined by General Conference, and by a portion of the receipts from World Communion Sunday.
- the Hispanic, Asian, and Native Americans Fund (HANA), supported by an apportionment and by receipts from World Communion Sunday.
- the Africa University, supported through apportionments and also as a World Service Special.

The United Methodist Student Loan Fund and the United Methodist Scholarship Fund. United Methodists attending college are eligible for the church's loan and scholarship program. The loan program, the oldest and largest church program of its type in the country, started in 1872, with offerings taken in Sunday schools. Today the fund lends more than $1.7 million a year.

Scholarships came more recently, beginning in 1945. By 1988, the church was awarding close to $1.8 million in scholarships each year.

All United Methodist college students are eligible for loans from the church, no matter which college they attend. Scholarships are awarded to students attending United Methodist colleges. Offerings from United Methodist Student Day support both loans and scholarships, and are divided equally between them.

The *Discipline* links the Annual Conference Board to the church's loan and scholarship program this way:

To promote the use of the United Methodist Loan Fund and to designate appropriate persons to represent the United Methodist Loan Fund on campuses, such persons normally being the Wesley Foundation Directors or ecumenical campus ministers supported by the Annual Conference; to provide the Office of Loans and Scholarships with the names and addresses of those persons; and to apprise students of alternative ways to apply for loans in the event there is no campus minister. [par. 732.4a(14)]

To administer the scholarship funds rebated to the annual conference by the Office of Loans and Scholarships in accordance with the guidelines of that office. [par. 732.4a(15)]

Ways to promote the fund are listed below. But three items from those paragraphs of the *Discipline* should be emphasized here. Campus ministers normally administer the United Methodist Loan Fund. But the Annual Conference Board must both inform them and send their names to the Office of Loans and Scholarships. That should be done with each change of campus ministry staff, and done early enough that students seeking loans will not be delayed.

Where there are no campus ministers, loans are still available. A pastor near the campus might serve as loan officer. The Board chair or treasurer might, as well. However it is handled, consult with the Office of Loans and Scholarships to get clearance. Then, use the conference newsletter or a general mailing to let all pastors know how to advise their students about obtaining a loan.

The Board may fund its own scholarship program, using money rebated to it from the Office of Loans and Scholarships. The Office rebates ten percent of the conference's Student Day offering to the Board for that purpose (twenty percent if the conference offering is $40,000 or more). The Board has considerable flexibility in administering those loans. However, there are some guidelines. Begin by contacting the Office of Loans and Scholarships for them.

The church relies upon the Annual Conference Board to publicize the Student Day offering and to encourage students and parents to apply for loans and scholarships. The Division of Higher Education and the Office of Loans and Scholarships supply program guidance and promotional materials. Here are some facts and ideas to keep in mind to help promote and administer the program of loans and scholarships in your annual conference.

1. The Office of Loans and Scholarships has brochures explaining loans and scholarships and telling how to apply for them. They are available in quantity. Send them routinely to all pastors and local church chairs of Higher Education and Campus Ministry.

2. The booklet, *College Bound*, carries complete loan and scholarship information, as well as information about all United Methodist schools and colleges and about government financial aid. Copies are available free to each local church.

3. The Office of Loans and Scholarships produces worship materials for use on United Methodist Student Day—including a litany, bulletin inserts, and offering envelopes. The materials are undated and may be used at any time during the year. Encourage local churches each year to get materials and to take a Student Day offering. The suggested date for the offering is the Sunday following Thanksgiving.

4. United Methodist scholarships are administered by United Methodist colleges and are available only to United Methodist students. Those who plan to attend church-related colleges should speak with the chaplain, the admissions officer, or the financial aid officer for information. Remind students to apply.

5. A yearly report is sent to each Annual Conference Board, showing the amount given by the annual conference to the Loan and Scholarship Fund. It also shows the amount awarded to students who come from the annual conference. Annual conferences usually receive two to three times more in loans and scholarships each year than they raise in their offerings. Report that information in the conference newsletter, accompanying it with photographs of some of the current year's recipients.

The Black College Fund. The Black College Fund carries on a mission begun by Methodists in 1872. In that year, the Freedman's Aid Society established a fund for the education of Black Americans. The Society was originated and supported by contributions from individual members of the Methodist Episcopal Church. But the fund quickly became a benevolence program of the entire church.

During its early years, the Society established and supported nearly 60 schools, many of them the only schools available to Blacks following the Civil War. Some of them— elementary and secondary schools, for the most part—gradually merged with the slowly developing public school system. Others—principally colleges—merged with each other.

Today, eleven historically Black colleges remain in the United Methodist Church's family of institutions. They continue to be among the most successful of all institutions educating Black Americans. Those colleges are:

• Bennett College, Greensboro, North Carolina
• Bethune-Cookman College, Daytona Beach, Florida
• Claflin College, Orangeburg, South Carolina
• Clark-Atlanta University, Atlanta, Georgia
• Dillard University, New Orleans, Louisiana
• Huston-Tillotson College, Austin, Texas
• Meharry Medical College, Nashville, Tennessee
• Paine College, Augusta, Georgia
• Philander Smith College, Little Rock, Arkansas
• Rust College, Holly Springs, Mississippi
• Wiley College, Marshall, Texas

The United Methodist Church has been and continues to be a pioneer in education for Blacks. It supports its commitment through the Black College Fund, which is an apportionment adopted each quadrennium by the General Conference. Each annual conference and local church, in turn, is apportioned its share.

How can Annual Conference Boards assist the Black College Fund? There are several ways:

1. Publicize the apportionment and encourage local churches to pay theirs in full.
2. Invite a Lina H. McCord Student Itinerant to your annual conference. The McCord Itinerants are all students from United Methodist Black colleges. For ten weeks each summer, they visit jurisdictions, speaking to annual conferences, visiting churches, and attending summer camps. The annual conference must provide room, meals, and transportation; all other expenses are covered by the Black College Fund.
3. Spread information about the Black colleges. The Black College Fund has leaflets, interpretive brochures, and reports, all suitable for distributing to local churches. Most are available either free or at very low cost.
4. Invite the presidents, admissions officers, and choirs of the Black colleges to attend annual conference. Urge your conference to adopt one of the colleges.
5. Be alert to students in your annual conference who would be good applicants for the Black colleges. Make certain they have the names and addresses of all eleven.

The Office of the Black College Fund also manages one other program of special interest to annual conferences: Minority In-Service Training (MIST). MIST funds are used to develop ethnic minority leadership for the church. They underwrite supervised training in campus ministry, teaching, advocacy, and more. Boards may write proposals for MIST funds or encourage their church colleges and campus ministries to do so. Obtain guidelines and application forms from the Office of the Black College Fund. MIST is supported by the World Communion Sunday offering.

Hispanic, Asian, and Native American Fund (HANA). In 1976 the General Conference instituted HANA—a fund to increase higher education among Hispanics, Asians, and Native Americans. Its primary vehicle is scholarships, made available to college juniors and seniors and to graduate students. Those students must be United Methodist and must be committed to leadership in the society and churches of their ethnic community. Annual Conference Boards play an important part in HANA by identifying potential leaders in those ethnic communities. Alert church-related colleges, campus ministries, and local congregations to forward names of candidates to the Division of Higher Education or to the Office of Loans and Scholarships. The Division has guidelines, brochures, and application forms.

HANA funds come from the World Communion Sunday offering. Take advantage of that Special Day to introduce HANA recipients to the annual conference, using the conference newsletter or a special mailing. Encourage the local church chair for Higher Education and Campus Ministry to use World Communion Sunday for an interpretive event. Guest speakers and explanatory materials would help. The Board could also assemble a worship packet with prayers, litanies, and hymns from the Hispanic, Asian, and Native American traditions.

The Africa University. General Conference, in 1988, adopted a dramatic new project. Although Methodist-related missions have been in Africa for many years, the church has no college or university there. General Conference remedied that. It voted to join with African United Methodists to build a university.

To give substance to its vote, the General Conference decided to raise $20 million in one quadrennium to finance the first phase of the building and to provide scholarships.

The money is to be raised in two ways. One-half, $10 million, became part of the World Service budget. That half is apportioned to each annual conference and local church. The remaining $10 million is to be raised as a World Service Special.

The Annual Conference Board, along with the conference Council on Ministries, must help kindle the local church's commitment to apportioned giving. Apportionments form the financial bedrock of the denomination's mission. Congregations must see them, not as dues, but as transfusions of faith and service. The Africa University has the potential to awaken just that understanding in the local church.

The World Service Special obliges the Board to think beyond apportionments. What will capture the interest of members of local churches for the Africa University? What will stir the imagination of the conference? How can this become more than a fund raiser? How can the project itself become vivid to the church?

The Annual Conference Board will work with the conference Council on Ministries to do conference-wide promotions of the Africa project. As it does, it will find resources available through United Methodist Communications and the General Board of Higher Education and Ministry. Through them, the Board can arrange for speakers, displays, brochures, videos, news releases, resources for articles, and other educational materials.

Services of the Division of Higher Education for the Annual Conference Program in Higher Education and Campus Ministry

The Division of Higher Education aids the Annual Conference Board in many ways. Several have already been mentioned—grants, scholarships, and promotional materials. But there are others.

As a part of its work with Annual Conference Boards and with colleges and campus ministries, the Division offers several kinds of services. They are: consultation, training, resources, research, and funding. Each is available to the Annual Conference Board. Here, briefly, is what they include.

Consultation. The Division offers consulting services, at no cost, to Annual Conference Boards, campus ministries, and church-related colleges. The services cover a wide range. Some, in each area, are:

Campus Ministry
on-site evaluation
administrative and program development
staff and personnel development
public policy
ecumenical covenants and agreements
student work and student movements
women's programs
ethnic minority programs
financing
legal consultation

Church-Related Schools and Colleges
presidential searches
administration
finances
church-relations
accreditation
academic development
legal consultation
public policy
investments
insurance

Annual Conference Boards
planning
administration
campus ministry and college relations
program development
finances
public policy
connectional relations
loans and scholarships
special programs and "Special Days"
legal consultation
district and local church training

Resources. The Division of Higher Education produces several ongoing resources—newsletters, bulletin inserts, informational pieces, and directories. Although each is targeted for a specific constituency, almost all are sent to the chairs of Annual Conference Boards of Higher Education and Campus Ministry. Others are available upon request.

Campus Ministry
Campus Ministry Directory
Keepin' in Touch (campus ministry newsletter)
Orientation magazine
Bible Studies for Students
Advent and Lenten meditation booklets for students
Singing the Songs of Zion in a New Land: The Psalms for a First-Year Student
Study Papers on Campus Ministry
Directory of United Methodist-Related Black Campus Ministers and Chaplains

Church-Related Schools and Colleges
Directory of Chief Executive Officers
Presidential Papers
College Bound
Access
Lex Collegii (newsletter on legal issues)
i.e. (international education)

Annual Conference Boards
New Perspectives (newsletter for Boards)
Black College Fund Newsletter
Loans and Scholarships Annual Report
Support for Higher Education (an annual statistical report of annual conference support
  for campus ministry and for church-related schools and colleges)
Access
Handbook for Higher Education and Campus Ministry in the Annual Conference

The Annual Conference Board will receive several of the campus ministry and schools and colleges materials automatically. The Division also publishes, as needed, books and booklets, brochures and reports, handbooks and resource packets. Many of those are also sent to Board chairs automatically. All will be listed in *New Perspectives* and may be requested from the Division.

Training. Training occupies a prominent place in the Division's agenda. Much of its training goes on through consultative services, where it is tailored to fit the needs of individual institutions. But the Division also sponsors workshops, institutes, and seminars to train new leaders and to deal with more general topics. Here are some.

Campus Ministry
New Campus Ministers' Orientation
Campus Ministry Skills Workshop
Student Forum
Black Campus Ministers
Special events for Hispanic, Asian, and Native American campus ministers

Church-Related Schools and Colleges
Institute of Higher Education
Seminar for Presidents and Spouses
New Presidents' Orientation
Public Policy Briefings

Annual Conference Boards
Jurisdictional Training Events
Annual Conference Board Training (available to each annual conference on request)
Mid-Quadrennium Consultations
Key Persons Consultation on Public Policy

Funding. In addition to loans and scholarships, the Division also funds annual conference programs. One way it channels support to them has already been mentioned: Minority In-Service Training (MIST)—managed through the Office of the Black College Fund. Campus ministries, church-related colleges, and Annual Conference Boards are all eligible for those moneys.

In addition, the Division, each year, invites all of its constituents to apply for grants under its appropriations program. The money underwrites new programs and cannot be used for equipment purchase, capital improvements, salary, or travel. Application forms and guidelines are sent to Annual Conference Boards, campus ministries, United

Methodist colleges, and to all bishops and Conference Council directors.

Research. The Division maintains a program of research and development, the Methodist Interactive Database System (MINDS). The system now collects data from annual conferences and church-related colleges. An annual report is sent to all Annual Conference Board chairs, listing each conference and showing its financial support for ministries in higher education. Research and development services available to constituents of the Division are:

- annual statistical reports on higher education support by annual conferences and jurisdictions;
- other higher education information (enrollment trends, denominational longitudinal analyses) as available and on request;
- consultation for research projects;
- financial analyses of schools and colleges (confidential and available only to institutions).

The Administrative Assignments of the Annual Conference Board of Higher Education and Campus Ministry

Earlier, mention was made to two responsibilities the Board administers on behalf of the Division of Higher Education:

- counseling institutions about property and endowments and maintaining trust and reversionary clauses
- conferring with GBHEM in the event any educational institution, Wesley Foundation, or other campus ministry moves to sever or modify its connection with the church or to violate the rules adopted by the Division of Higher Education.

The following paragraphs identify some of the issues involved in those responsibilities. However, each is complex and ought to be addressed with the advice of the legal counsel of the annual conference and of the Division of Higher Education.

Counseling institutions about property and endowments entrusted to the institutions. The Board gives counsel when it expresses the attitudes and advice of the annual conference to an institution. Counsel does not deal with legalities. When schools and colleges receive endowments (sums of money to be invested, the earnings from which support the college) and property for specific purposes, the institution is bound to observe those purposes. That is a legality.

But money and property may have been given by the church or by individuals without restriction, yet with an interest in supporting, for example, religious programs. When college programs change, as they must, the advice and counsel of the Board should help the college decide other acceptable uses for those funds.

Enforcing trust and reversionary clauses. Trusts are monies given to institutions for purposes designated by the donor; often only the earnings from trusts may be used.

Reversionary clauses are statements that trusts or properties will revert to the donor in the event the institution changes its mission or dissolves.

The United Methodist Church asks all institutions which it has founded to include reversionary clauses in their bylaws. Many have. In the event of institutional change, the church directs the Division of Higher Education to protect the church's assets, which includes enforcing reversionary clauses. The Annual Conference Board is an important part of the process. The *Discipline* instructs the Division to:

Take such action as is necessary to protect or recover resources, property, and investments of The United Methodist Church, or any Conference, agency, or institution thereof, in capital or endowment funds of any educational institution, Wesley Foundation, or campus ministry founded, organized, developed, or assisted under the direction or with the cooperation of The United Methodist Church should any such institution discontinue operation or move to sever or modify its connection with the church or violate the terms of any rules adopted by the Board or the terms of any such grant of new capital or endowment funds made by The United Methodist Church or any Conference, agency, or institution thereof. . . . In the event any such educational institution, Wesley Foundation, or other campus ministry unit shall endeavor to discontinue operation or move to sever or modify its connection with the church or violate the rules adopted by the division in accordance with Par. 1516.3b, it shall be the duty of the trustees and the administrators of such institutions, along with the Conference agency on higher education and the resident bishop of the Conference in which such institution is located, to confer at the earliest possible opportunity with appropriate representatives of the division to determine what resources and aid the division may be able to provide and to permit the division to carry out its responsibilities under this paragraph. (par.1516.3c.)

The Board should request copies of the charters and bylaws of all church-related schools and colleges and of all of the campus ministries it supports, take note of those that do have reversionary clauses, and begin conversations with those that do not. That does not mean that ecumenical campus ministries must agree to a reversionary clause; it does mean that United Methodist trusts and capital must be protected. Similarly, there may be some colleges that are not owned by the church but which choose to work in relationship to it. Reversion clauses may not always be appropriate in those cases; but again, there should be discussion about the protection of United Methodist trusts or capital.

In all cases, other than seeking information, the Board should request the assistance of its annual conference legal counsel and of the Division of Higher Education.

Conferring with the appropriate representatives of the General Board of Higher Education and Ministry. When it is clear that the connection between an educational institution or campus ministry and the church is going to change, the Board should immediately contact the associate general secretary of the Division of Higher Education. Among the kinds of changes included are:

1. A United Methodist school or college seeking to change its mission;
2. A United Methodist school or college seeking to sever its connection to the church;
3. A United Methodist school or college deciding to close;
4. A Wesley Foundation Board merging with an ecumenical ministry apart from approval by the Annual Conference Board;
5. A Wesley Foundation Board selling its property or other major assets without approval of the Annual Conference Board;
6. A Wesley Foundation closing without approval of the Annual Conference Board;
7. The dissolution of an ecumenical campus ministry in which United Methodist assets are contested;
8. The withdrawal of support by ecumenical partners from an ecumenical campus ministry that has received a grant from the Division of Higher Education.

The Division works closely with its own legal counsel and with the University Senate. Through its resources, it will be able to assist the Annual Conference Board and to fulfill its own responsibilities under the *Discipline.*

Conclusion

The Annual Conference Board and the Division of Higher Education enrich and complement each other's ministries. The Division is able to pool church-wide resources and information for the benefit of the annual conference. The annual conference maintains a close, day-by-day contact with educational institutions on behalf of the church.

The Division's programs of consultation, funding, training, research, and resources are for the quickening and strengthening of ministry in higher education—schools and colleges, campus ministries, local churches. Its scholarships are for the training of leaders for the church and for the world. In all cases, its effectiveness depends greatly on the Annual Conference Board. It seeks consistently to be of service to that Board for the sake of the ministry they share together.

Chapter Eight

The Organization And Membership Of The Annual Conference Board Of Higher Education And Campus Ministry

At present, Annual Conference Boards of Higher Education and Campus Ministry differ greatly in their organization and membership. Some are small; some are large. Many have several standing committees, a few have none at all. And some are themselves subcommittees or divisions of larger Boards.

The same holds for patterns of membership. Some Boards have only a few members who serve in colleges or campus ministries; others are almost entirely composed of such people. Some do not allow campus ministers and church-relations officers membership with voice and vote; others do. Some have primarily representatives from each district; others use a different principle of selection.

Further, in areas where two or more annual conferences own colleges or campus ministries in common, they sometimes merge to form an Area Commission on Higher Education and Campus Ministry. Annual Conference Boards may assign many of their duties to Area Commissions and become their annual conference's chief representatives on them. But, since Area Commissions relate principally to campus ministries and colleges, the Board still needs an organization and membership to work with public policy and with districts and local churches, and to present its programs to the annual conference.

Which structure is best? What is the ideal membership for the Annual Conference Board? Answers to questions like those grow best from an understanding of each annual conference, of its colleges and campus ministries, and of the public policy issues it faces. This chapter will suggest some useful patterns of organization. It will also describe some ways to determine the membership of the Annual Conference Board.

Before considering those matters, however, the Board should consider the relationship between two factors: program and administration. They are the two kinds of work the Board will spend most of its time doing. And between them they affect the shape of the Board and the kinds of members it will need.

Two Key Factors: Administration and Program

Boards tend to organize along the path of greatest familiarity. That often means they become heavy on administration and light on program. But both factors are essential—the trick is to find a balance that serves the mission of the Board.

To begin with, the Board's greatest interest is program. Program is to the Board what a prepared meal is to a recipe book: the aim and proof of its value. Administration is to the Board what grocery shopping is to the meal: the selection and management of the best ingredients. The problem besetting many Boards is their excessive devotion of time to administration.

And the flaw that gives rise to the problem itself arises from a simple confusion. That confusion is between administrative functions and administrative committees. Often Boards create a committee for each administrative function. When they do, that leaves meager means for managing program.

For example, a Board that has campus ministries and church-related schools and colleges in its conference may find that it has several administrative tasks to perform. Among them, property, budget and finance, personnel, scholarship management and awards, long-range planning, nominations, policy formation, fund raising, and more. The temptation in the Board is often to deal with these by establishing several administrative standing committees. The list could be quite long: property committee, finance committee, personnel committee, nominating committee, long-range planning committee, fund-raising committee, and so on.

Once the Board assigns members to those committees, it has a large remainder of work unaccounted for: programs in campus ministry, colleges and universities, public policy, district and local church development, and general church projects. Who will tend to those?

The question is serious. Boards have limited time and budget, and must stretch both to cover an enormous range. They must do their administrative work. But that work cannot exhaust the Board's time and energy. In fact, the relationship should be the reverse. Administration should empower program. Program should drive decisions about administration.

For that reason, it is best to think of administrative *functions* first, and only of administrative *committees* afterwards. Each administrative function does not need its own administrative committee. In fact, some functions do not need administrative committees at all. In many cases, administrative functions fit quite naturally into the province of a program committee. If so, why not lodge them there?

Think, for example, of the administrative function of property care. In most annual conferences the only property cared for by the Board is campus ministry property. Or think of personnel. In many conferences, again, the only professional personnel under the Board's supervision are campus ministers. In those cases, why not lodge those functions with a program committee on campus ministry?

Even when a function affects two program areas, it can be placed with program committees. Nominations are a case in point. The Annual Conference Board nominates members of Wesley Foundation Boards. It also, in some places, has a role in nominating or confirming college trustees. Those two tasks are distinct. The schools and colleges committee could see to the trustees; the campus ministry committee could see to the Wesley Foundation Board.

Sometimes it isn't clear where an administrative task falls. But even then, it doesn't necessarily require its own committee. Many conferences have scholarship funds. They usually require both promotional activities and handling of mechanical details. The schools and colleges committee could handle that—especially if the scholarships are restricted to students at United Methodist colleges. But the campus ministry committee might be asked to handle scholarships, which could then be administered by campus ministers and chaplains, much as they handle loans now. Or, because students from local churches will receive the scholarships, the task might fit the hands of the committee working with districts and local churches.

Putting administrative functions in tandem with programs will keep them close to the people who know the program best. Sights will set first on program, and free up time and energy for it. Those are the happy results of realizing that administrative functions don't always require administrative committees.

But administrative committees will still be needed. The size of a Board and its program will determine its administrative needs. But other factors need to be kept in mind. Some functions require balancing needs from one program area against those from another. Others may consume so much time that they would devour the agenda of a program committee. In some Boards, budget and finance have those characteristics. They often, therefore, have their own separate committee.

Three questions should help Boards decide how to distribute administrative functions:

1. What are our important program areas?
2. Which administrative functions could be assigned to program committees?
3. Which administrative functions (if any) require a committee of their own?

Boards will answer those questions differently. And, during the course of a quadrennium, some functions may shift from one committee to another. But the principles that direct the placement ought to remain clear: administration empowers program, program drives administration.

Organization

Organization, like membership, depends greatly on the annual conference and the scope of the Board's program. One annual conference may contain several colleges and campus ministries and deal with yearly budgets exceeding $1 million. Another may have no colleges and do all of its campus ministry ecumenically. No single structure would fit those two extremes or all of the variations between them.

Further, some conferences work through Area Commissions—agencies, as we noted earlier, that relate to United Methodist colleges and/or campus ministries on behalf of two or more conferences. Although Area Commissions have only the responsibilities given them by the Annual Conference Boards, once those Commissions exist, the Board has to build structures to work with them. They are important variables in decisions about the organization of the Annual Conference Board.

The following paragraphs will describe three common ways Annual Conference Boards are now organized. Even these have several variations in practice. But they supply a basis for thinking about what will match both the needs of your conference and the scope of your program. Each also represents a different solution to the problem of balancing program and administrative tasks.

A fourth plan of organization will follow those, one built to suggest a way to blend some administrative functions into the program areas of the Board.

Committee of the Whole.

In annual conferences that have few campus ministries (or primarily ecumenical campus ministries) and no more than one church-related college, Annual Conference Boards tend to function as committees of the whole: everyone participates in all phases of the program, and all decisions are made by the entire group.

Boards that function as a whole often have executive committees to set the agenda, deal with matters that emerge between meetings, and prepare the budgets. But their principal work—campus ministry, college relations, scholarships, Student Day—enlists the participation of each member.

When the work demand spreads beyond normal limits, these Boards rely on task groups—temporary committees to do research or suggest programs. But task groups are not decision-making bodies. They function on behalf of the Board, and the Board, after considering their reports, makes its decisions as a body of the whole.

Standing Committees.

When Boards increase the scope of their programs or have larger numbers of campus ministries and/or church-related colleges to work with, they expand their structure. The most common change is to create standing committees, permanent committees that carry out several of the Board's ongoing functions. The Board remains primary; committees routinely report to the Board; most decisions are made by the Board. But a great deal of the thought, research, and budget building for areas of the Board's work begins in the committees.

The most common standing committees are:

- Campus Ministry Committee
- Higher Education Committee
- Finance Committee
- Executive Committee

Some Boards, in order to adapt to their annual conference's needs, may also create task groups or standing committees on long-range planning, personnel, emerging ministries, and property.

Divisions.

In some annual conferences, especially those with several church-related colleges and many campus ministries, Boards have formed divisions.

The most common divisions are:

- Division of Campus Ministry
- Division of Higher Education

Because the scope of the work is large, the number of institutions great, and the budget large, the Board as a whole does not have the time to attend to or vote on everything. Consequently, divisions are given a good deal of authority, usually having to bring only matters of budget, policy, and long-range planning to the entire Board for approval.

To coordinate divisions, the Boards place great reliance on an executive committee. That committee, composed of members of both divisions, makes decisions in between meetings, manages the process of budget building, represents both divisions in the conference Council on Ministries and conference Council on Finance and Administration, and creates other committees and task forces for the work of the Board.

Some structural decisions Boards have to make when they work as divisions are:

1. **Is personnel a function of a division or of the Board?** For example, Wesley Foundations have full-time campus ministers, support other employees, and have elected Board members. Where in the structure should personnel matters that relate to the bishop and cabinet be placed? Where should the policies governing hiring of support persons be vested? Who should take responsibility for nominating the Wesley Foundation Board of Directors?

2. **Are scholarships a function of a division or of the Board?** Annual conferences receive enough money through the Student Day offering to fund scholarships. They may also have conference scholarship funds to administer. Who should promote and grant scholarships?

3. **Who will take responsibility for special days and offerings for higher education?** Along with that, who will interpret the Black College Fund and the Hispanic, Asian, and Native American Fund (HANA)?

4. **Who will be responsible for public policy issues?**

5. **Who will be responsible for building the budget?**

6. **Who will deal with property?** Boards have some slight relationship to college property but often a major one to campus ministry buildings. Should policies for maintenance of property, liability coverage, and use become the work of the entire Board, or a committee, or be handled by divisions?

Program Committees.

Another possible structure for Annual Conference Boards is based on a fuller estimate of their programmatic work. Variations are possible for conferences with large or small numbers of institutions and campus ministries. The basic pattern is that of the Board with standing committees. In this case, however, the standing committees correspond to the program the Board—its missional and connectional program.

At least four standing committees will have programs to develop and monitor:

- Schools, Colleges, and Universities
- Campus Ministry
- Public Policy
- Connectional Relations (annual conference, district and local church)

Other committees are optional—executive committee, finance committee, property committee, or personnel committee. Whether they are needed depends upon how much responsibility the Board wishes to assign the program committees. If the only property the Board deals with, for example, is a Wesley Foundation building, property matters may well be assigned to the campus ministry committee. Connectional relations committees may handle scholarships. And the chairs of each may form a task group on budget, finance, or agenda. The two emphases of this plan of organization are program and flexible administration.

Membership

Most annual conferences have policies on organization to assure that every Board has a balanced membership. Beyond that, Boards can play an active part in recruiting and nominating their members. That holds especially for ex officio members, but also for persons elected directly by the annual conference. Boards need members who can get work done effectively and knowledgeably. To accomplish that, they may write their rules of organization to include strategic persons. Those rules may even become a part of the conference nominating procedure.

As it makes plans for membership, the Board should consider three categories. They are: members from the districts; representatives from campus ministries, schools, and colleges; and people with needed expertise.

Membership from the Districts.

Annual Conference Boards may have members drawn from each district of the conference. If Boards can connect with those who plan and carry out district programs, the work of both can be greatly enhanced.

As a Board organizes, it should survey the church groups organized in the districts. Which have interests in common? Which have so much in common that they should have persons serve either as full or ex officio members of the Board? Among those to think about are the district Council on Youth Ministries, the Young Adult Council, United Methodist Men, and United Methodist Women.

Usually, the most important agency is the district Council on Ministries. The Council integrates all of the district programs and, in addition, plans and sponsors others. It is one place that gives access to programs aimed at the local church.

Activities of the Annual Conference Board become more effective when they radiate through the groups represented on the Council. The Council becomes stronger when it adds to its resources those the Board makes available through its colleges and campus ministries. With that in mind, Boards may create provisions in their rules of organization for each district to have one person who is a member of the Annual Conference Board and of the district Council on Ministries.

Institutional Representatives.

Most Annual Conference Boards have Wesley Foundations, church-related schools and colleges, or ecumenical campus ministries within their boundaries. In addition, some have colleges or campus ministries outside their conference boundaries to which they have a special relationship. The question often arises as to how the Boards can keep informed well enough to truly represent those institutions. The answer most have come to is to invite campus ministries and church-related colleges to have membership on the Board or to give Board representatives some form of interaction with the college or campus ministry.

One approach is for the Board to include in its membership the campus ministers from Wesley Foundations (and, occasionally, United Methodist campus ministers serving ecumenical units located within the annual conference) and either the presidents, church-relations officers, or chaplains from the church-related colleges it supports. This approach has been criticized in recent years for fostering possible conflicts of interest. It places campus ministers and college personnel in the position of voting on the grants they are to be the recipients of, on the policies of the conference for the governance of its programs with them, and, in some events, on the salaries that will benefit them personally.

Another approach allows for representation but arranges it differently. Since the *Discipline* tells the Annual Conference Board to hold the Wesley Foundation Board responsible for adhering to conference policy, one person is made a member of both. That person may be chosen from the Annual Conference Board and assigned to a Wesley Board or from the Wesley Board and assigned to serve on the Annual Conference Board.

A conference that supports ecumenical campus ministry may provide for cross-representation. Where there are state ecumenical commissions, Board members may be assigned to represent the conference on those commissions. That ensures good two-way communication.

Where there is no state commission and the annual conference supports local ecumenical campus ministries directly, Annual Conference Board members who live close to those ministries may serve as representatives to them. Or, as with Wesley Foundations, the local ecumenical ministry may select a United Methodist member to serve on the Annual Conference Board.

Annual Conference Boards also need good communication with their church-related colleges. They may routinely invite the president of the college, the church-relations officer, or the chaplain to attend their meetings. Some Boards give those persons full membership. But there are other arrangements. One conference has a College Council, a group to advise the Board on matters pertaining to the colleges, composed of college administrators and Annual Conference Board members. In another conference, the Annual Conference Board chair sits on the church-relations committee of the college's trustees. Annual conferences that elect trustees to colleges may invite a college trustee to membership on the Annual Conference Board.

For sustaining close ties to institutions, nothing substitutes for knowing names and faces, for getting information first hand, and for planning together. The point that calls for careful consideration is: who should be asked? Should it be professionals from the institutions—campus ministers, presidents, church-relations officers, and chaplains? Should it be appointed delegates from the Annual Conference Board? Should it be the nonprofessional elected governors of the institutions—college trustees, Wesley Foundation Board members, ecumenical representatives?

The most sound administrative solution is for elected members of colleges, campus ministries, and Annual Conference Boards to be the connecting links. Place college trustees and members of campus ministry boards of directors on the Annual Conference Board. Invite the professionals—presidents, campus ministers, church-relations officers—

when their expertise is needed. Three advantages of this solution are: 1) it relates Board to Board, the Annual Conference Board working directly with those most responsible for the institutions: their boards of trustees and directors; 2) it allows for the presence of knowledgeable persons on the Annual Conference Board; and 3) it does not put professionals in the embarrassing position of voting on their own budgets and salaries.

Persons with Special Expertise.

Annual Conference Boards need members with experience in higher education. Not that only higher education professionals should be members. The Board also benefits from expertise in other fields. But the world of higher education is complex, and ministering within it requires some special skills and training. The Board will benefit from the presence of experienced members.

While the membership of Annual Conference Boards must be decided within each annual conference, these questions will help test the versatility and adequacy of their membership categories.

1. Do we have members who are graduates of United Methodist schools, colleges, or universities? The Board plays a major part in interpreting the church-related colleges within its conference boundaries. It also is the primary representative of all 125 United Methodist educational institutions. Graduates can tell about those schools from firsthand experience.
2. Do we have staff, faculty, or trustees from church-related colleges? Where the Annual Conference Board relates to church colleges within its own boundaries, it will be expected to know a good deal about them. When the colleges have representation on the Board, the Board learns more and interprets more effectively.
3. Do we have teachers or administrators from public higher education? Much of the Board's work takes place on public campuses. Those campuses also educate great numbers of United Methodist students. The Board will move more efficiently on public campuses if it has the guidance of persons who know their organization, atmosphere, and opportunities.
4. Do we have members who have participated in campus ministry as students or who participate now as faculty or administrators? Those who have at-hand experience can help other members of the Board understand what campus ministry means to people on the campus.
5. Do we have members who are former campus ministry professionals or Wesley Foundation Board members? Again, there can be great value in the views of those who have governed and directed the work of ministry on public campuses. Those persons will provide a useful historical perspective for interpreting campus work.
6. Do we have members with experience in state and federal public policy issues? To a large extent, the prospects for higher education hang on state and federal legislation and policy. The consequences of tax reform and higher education legislation will be felt in the home of nearly every family that has hopes for a college education. The *Discipline* asks the Annual Conference Board to interact with public higher education and to assist institutions with their relations with the state. Among those relations are those that undergird both private and public higher education.

7. Do we have members who have been recipients of United Methodist loans and scholarships? The loan and scholarship funds of The United Methodist Church have helped thousands of students finance their education. They are only one part, although a very significant one, of the student support made available through the church. Those who have been helped by the funds could become useful interpreters and might also take a special interest in United Methodist Student Day—the day when offerings are received to underwrite the loan and scholarships funds.

Annual Conference Boards do not have to answer yes to all these questions. The composition of the Board should be determined by the makeup of the annual conference and the dimensions of its program in higher education. However, the questions do suggest the kinds of special knowledge and background that could magnify the effectiveness of the Board.

Conclusion

Both membership and structure are important considerations for the Annual Conference Board of Higher Education and Campus Ministry. Decisions about both will affect the quality and quantity of work the Board can do. Members should be chosen both on the basis of their broad representation of the church and their specific knowledge and experience. Structures should be adopted that match the mission and ambition of the Board and the needs of the annual conference.

The primary factor, however, is program. What needs to be done? How can it be done? The next chapter introduces a system of planning that will help answer these questions.

Chapter Nine

Planning The Annual Conference Ministry In Higher Education

This chapter describes a six step planning process for Annual Conference Boards of Higher Education and Campus Ministry. It involves:

- assessing the present
- expressing the future
- determining support
- creating structures
- assigning responsibilities
- evaluating

One value of the six step process is that it can be spread over more than one year. With the limited time most Boards have to manage programs operating in the present, they might well need more than one year to plan for the future.

The plan lends itself to a retreat setting. Step One is optional. Steps Two and Three can be done at a retreat. Steps Four and Five can be done either at the retreat or during an extended follow-up meeting.

Another value is that some of the steps can be used each year afterward for ongoing evaluation. Once information is on hand and a pattern has been established for sorting it into categories, Boards can measure their progress.

Successful evaluation must have more than hearsay and hunch as its basis. Here is one way to put it on more solid ground.

Step One: Assess the Present

Boards often oversee their programs, but seldom oversee themselves. Good planning begins with self-scrutiny. We can learn a lot by looking at ourselves. Assessing the present does that, so long as it doesn't become a labor of morbid fault finding.

The best way to start is by getting as objective a list as possible of what the Board has actually been doing. It may surprise you.

Start by listing the Board's programs in the following areas:

Campus Ministry
Schools, Colleges, and Universities

Public Policy
Annual Conference
District
Local Church
Special Projects, such as:
    Scholarships
    Special Offerings
    Special Days (Student Day, for example)
    Advance Specials
Other

For each of those have one Board member prepare a brief statement (no more than a page or two in outline form) containing:

- highlights from the last four years of that program;
- projected and actual budgets from two of the last four years;
- a list of the personnel involved in that program both in the Annual Conference Board and in the area of ministry (campus minister, college staff person, local pastor, for example);
- descriptions of facilities if the ministry has a specific location, including their present state and adequacy.

Have the Board's executive committee describe the present organization of the Annual Conference Board of Higher Education and Campus Ministry. Make an organizational chart, showing how the Board is presently organized and where the responsibility for each of the following functions is lodged:

Campus Ministry
Schools, Colleges, and Universities
Public Policy
Annual Conference
District
Local Church
Special Programs:
    Scholarships Recruitment
    Special Days
    Advance Specials
    Others
Administration:
    Budget
    Evaluation of Program
    Evaluation and Placement of Personnel
    Property and Facilities
Liaison with:
    Cabinet
    Conference Council on Ministries

Conference Council on Finance and Administration
District Council on Ministries
Local Church Coordinator for Higher Education and Campus Ministry
State or District Ecumenical Campus Ministry Commission

In order to get a view of how the Board has done its work, select two major issues dealt with by the Board during the past four years. Describe step-by-step how the Board managed those problems, what its actual process of data gathering, analysis, and decision making was. Ask members and former members of the Board to help you. These directions will help reveal how the Board dealt with each issue:

1. State the issue.
2. Describe how it first came to the Board's attention.
3. How did the Board first respond?
4. What steps of analysis were undertaken to
   —gather facts?
   —get other pertinent data?
   —determine what the data meant?
   —evaluate the importance of the issue?
5. What committee of the Board received the data?
6. How were the data brought to the Board? To whom else were they brought?
7. What possible interpretations of the data did the Board consider?
8. What other agencies influenced the considerations?
9. What decision was made? Who made the decision?
10. How was the decision implemented?

This information should be shared with the full Board as the first step in its planning. Among other things, the members should be asked to detect ways the procedures used to deal with the issues described above matched the processes suggested by the Board's organization chart and its policies. In which ways did they vary? Did they influence the Board to alter its procedures, organization, or policies?

This is not for the purpose of finding fault. Attention ought to be on the processes that proved workable, on the activities that took the bulk of the Board's time and budget, and on programs and issues that still bulk large in the Board's agenda.

Step Two: Express the Future

Planning for the future should help the Board reverse its angle of vision. Rather than looking at where it wishes to go in the light of where it is, it will be able to look at where it is in the light of where it wants to go—viewing the valley from the mountain peak rather than the mountain peak from the valley.

Goals, well stated and broadly accepted, provide that perspective from the future. When groups move toward a desired future rather than simply through a muddled present, they know what counts as progress and what constitutes victory. Nonetheless, goals are not absolute. If goals move in one direction and history moves in quite another, the Board may find itself marooned on the mountain top, detached from actual events.

As it expresses the future, therefore, the Annual Conference Board of Higher Education and Campus Ministry must realize two things: Apart from clearly stated goals, there is no way to chart progress or justify decisions; and one goal of any group must be to constantly assess its goals in the face of new needs, new learnings, and new visions.

This step deals exclusively with discovering and stating goals. The entire six step planning process provides the occasion for adjustment and redirection.

Begin by preparing a list of programs the Board would like to have in place within three years for each of these program areas:

Campus Ministry
Schools, Colleges, and Universities
Public Policy
Annual Conference
District
Local Church
Special Programs:
    Scholarships and Recruitment
    Special Days
    Advance Specials
    Other

The list may include continuations of present programs as well as new ones. It can also include first steps of programs that will need more than three years to complete. *All programs should be specific to the program area and should be unfettered by financial considerations.* This may be done best in small groups, each group making a list of programs for one program area. You may wish to combine annual conference, district, and local church programs and assign them to one committee.

Have each committee prepare its list for presentation to the entire group. To do that the committees should sort out their suggested programs in the following way:

1. Identify all the proposed programs that the Board must carry out. The reason the programs must be carried out may vary—present commitments to persons or programs, expectations of the annual conference, imperatives of mission. But list those programs.

For each program that must be carried out, note the length of time the program is expected to last. Is it to phase out gradually, to be maintained and supported over the next several years, to increase in support?

Describe the "must" programs as they are to be in three years. Then, for each, state the major blocks of time and pieces of work that must be done leading up to that time. Put that information on a calendar, indicating which parts of the program must be in place by when. Then, break out the tasks that must be completed in the year ahead for each project, and write in detail every task that must be accomplished within that time. The procedure could look like this:

- Describe the full program as it is to be in three years. Include personnel, program activities, place or facilities, costs.
- Describe what must be accomplished by two-and-a-half years. Include personnel, program activities, etc.

- Describe what must be accomplished by two years, including personnel, etc.
- Describe what must be accomplished by one-and-a-half years, including personnel, etc.
- Describe what must be done by the end of this year. Break down this year's tasks and deadlines.

2. Identify those programs that are not "musts," but which should rank high among the Board's priorities. Such programs may matter a good deal to the Board and reach high in excitement and commitment. They may be new or continuing.

List those program ideas and, as above, describe where they should be in three years. Then break down the stages by which the program is to be assembled and note which major blocks would have to be done by when. Be most specific for parts of the program occurring in the year ahead. Use the calendar stages above to determine the schedule the Board will need to follow.

3. From among the remaining program suggestions, choose the most worthwhile and achievable. Follow the same steps for determining the work calendar for them.

The planning committees should bring their reports to the entire group. Once all have been heard, and all proposed programs are on newsprint for all to see, the entire group should reach agreement about the "must" programs and the other highest priority programs.

Following that, a composite calendar should be made. The calendar should show three or four years ahead, measured in three month blocks. It could be made of several sheets of newsprint and should be large enough for everyone to see. On that calendar place every "must" and high priority program, showing the schedule recommended by its planning committee.

Then have the group discuss three things:

- Is the total work load realistic for the Board?
- Which programs will demand the greatest amount of Board effort and energy?
- When will they require it?

If the answer to the first question is no, consider these questions:

a. Can any programs be delayed by one or two years, thereby shifting part of the work load to a later date?
b. Can any program be spread out over more than three years, thereby thinning out its demands on any one year?
c. Can the schedule for any program be compacted, thereby completing it before it conflicts with other program demands?

If the answers to a, b, and c, are no, identify those programs that most conflict for time. Then ask: Would the conflict be a problem if we were doing only these programs? If the answer is yes, a decision will have to be made about which of the programs must be curtailed or eliminated. If the answer is no, locate another program that has less priority for the Board; if it is eliminated will the congestion in scheduling be relieved? If not, move to the next lowest program. Continue until you have on the calendar only those programs that can realistically be achieved.

Step Three: Determine Support

Determining support for programs involves matching project costs with projected income. Much of this can be done by sending the accepted programs from Step Two back to the planning committees. Their work this time has three aspects:

- estimating program costs
- determining all sources of income
- assuring levels of support

First, for each of the programs remaining on the calendar from Step Two, have the committees estimate the total support needed in the categories below for each of the three years.

Year 1

Program (materials, etc.) _____
Personnel (salary and expenses)_____
Facilities_____
Administrative costs to the Board _____
   Total _____

Year 2

Program (materials, etc.) _____
Personnel (salary and expenses)_____
Facilities_____
Administrative costs to the Board _____
   Total _____

Year 3

Program (materials, etc.) _____
Personnel (salary and expenses)_____
Facilities_____
Administrative costs to the Board _____
   Total _____

In "Program" be certain to list costs of materials, equipment, transportation, and fees. In "Personnel" include such items as salary, benefits, car and travel allowance, training, and continuing education expenses. In "Facilities" include such items as parsonage or housing allowance, building construction and maintenance, utilities, permanent equipment, and projected long-term maintenance.

Next, determine all possible sources of income and estimate what they could bring in for each of the next three years. Include in this any money the program units (Board committees, campus ministries) are expected to raise for themselves.

Income from the Annual Conference

Year 1 _____   Year 2 _____   Year 3 _____

Income from Advance Specials

Year 1 _____   Year 2 _____   Year 3 _____

Income from special fund raising by the Annual Conference Board of Higher Education and Campus Ministry

Year 1 _____   Year 2 _____   Year 3 _____

Funds to be raised by the program committee responsible for this area
(Do a separate line for each committee or unit)

Year 1 _____   Year 2 _____   Year 3 _____

Endowment fund goals for each year

Year 1 _____   Year 2 _____   Year 3 _____

Endowment earnings projected for each year

Year 1 _____   Year 2 _____   Year 3 _____

Other special fund or United Methodist Foundation earnings

Year 1 _____   Year 2 _____   Year 3 _____

Income from grants

Year 1 _____   Year 2 _____   Year 3 _____

TOTAL

Year 1 _____   Year 2 _____   Year 3 _____

Again, the committees should report to the group. However, this time, instead of evaluating their suggestions, ask the whole group to add ideas about funding for each project.

The final stage of this process belongs to the executive committee of the Board. It must compute the costs and assess the sources of income for all of the programs. Its task is to prepare a final report to the group on what it believes are the programs and sources of support that are truly possible for the Board. In that process, the executive committee ought to consult with representatives of the conference Council on Finance and Administration and the conference Council on Ministries.

If income equals the projected costs of the programs, all is well. If not, either newer plans must be made for increasing income, or program priorities should be shifted. That becomes the agenda for the next full session of the Board. At that time, if program plans exceed time, talent, or money, tough decisions will have to be made. If they match, then the Board can proceed to the next step and begin to choose a structure to get its work done.

Step Four: Create Structures

Steps One, Two, and Three allow the Board to state clearly its present program, future program, and projected income. Decisions about the organization of the Board should be made in the light of that information. Chapter Eight outlined several patterns of organization. The following considerations will help the Board select a pattern for its own work.

First, it will be helpful to agree on a set of terms for discussing organization. In this section, these terms will be used:

MODEL. The *total* organizational pattern of the Board.

PROGRAM AREAS. The broad general areas in which the Board carries out its mission, such as campus ministry, public policy, schools and colleges, district and local church.

STRATEGY. The specific plan (organization and process) for managing any program area of the Board. For example, if the Board works in divisions, how will each division organize itself and carry out its work?

MANAGEMENT TASKS. The specific responsibilities the Board has for each of its program committees. How does the Board want each committee to deal with policy, personnel, property, and so on? Which policies, for example, must be adopted by the Board as a whole, and which may be made by the program committee? For a complete list of management tasks, see Chapter Two.

For example, the Board may decide to work as a committee of the whole, using task groups for special projects (Model). It may decide that church-related schools, colleges, and universities will become principal concerns (Program Area). It will then review the managerial roles the *Discipline* assigns it in that program area (Management Tasks). Finally, it will decide how to do its work in that program area—what specific programs to carry out, how to relate to the colleges, how to form its task forces for the work, what reporting procedures to use, etc. (Strategy).

1. Choosing a Model.

While there is no single recipe for producing the best organization, there are some considerations that help the choice and design. A model should show two things:

* the assignment of responsibilities within the Board;
* the relationship between those who are assigned different responsibilities.

To build a model, begin by listing the program areas in which the Board will be working.

Program Areas

_____	_____
_____	_____
_____	_____

Review the projected programs for each of those areas. Determine whether the supervision of those programs can be best managed by the Board working as a committee of the whole, or whether the total work load will require the Board to subdivide in some way.

If subdivision of some sort seems advisable, the Board has at least these options:

* Task Forces
* Standing Committees
* Divisions

The following questions should help the Board decide which kind of subdividing to try:

a. Are the program areas conceived as short-term or long-term projects?
b. Do the program areas involve the management of personnel, program, budget, property, and evaluation?
   —How many program areas require such management?
   —How many units in each program area require such management?
c. How much meeting time does the Board as a whole have each year?
   —Is it sufficient time to act as a committee of the whole?
   —Is it sufficient time to meet in task forces or standing committees?
   —Do some program areas presently consume the bulk of the Board's time?
   —Are there some areas the Board has not been able to work in because of time limitations?
d. In addition to program areas, which administrative functions must the Board maintain:

Finance	Personnel
Executive	Promotion
Evaluation	Others

—Which of those functions can be wed to program areas?

—Which will have to be managed by administrative committees?

—Will it be necessary for those committees to meet at times other than Board meetings?

—Will those responsible for program areas be needed in any of the committees?

Short-term programs require only task groups. If the Board is small and has no campus ministry units or church-related colleges, it may decide to work primarily with tasks groups and an executive committee.

Long-term programs usually benefit from specialized attention. If the Board is small but must relate closely and over the long haul to two or more institutions, standing committees may help it work more efficiently. That is especially true if it has no more than two campus ministries and no more than one church-related college within its annual conference.

If a Board has several campus ministries and relates to two or more church-related colleges, it may require two divisions, each with its own officers. It may also require task groups and standing committees to manage the other areas of its program (such as districts and local churches) and its administrative work. It is also possible to have subcommittees in divisions. For example, a division on schools and colleges might well have subcommittees on public policy and scholarships.

The model should show program areas and administrative responsibilities and designate the task force, standing committee, or division to which each is assigned.

The next step in building a model is to show how each of the task forces, standing committees, administrative committees, or divisions relates to the others, and how each relates to the whole. For that, some kind of a spatial design (flow chart, administrative graph) is often useful.

This portion of the model shows the Board's **PROCEDURES.** Procedures are agreements about how information is transmitted and decisions are made. When a Board works in task forces, standing committees, or divisions, it usually delegates some decisions to those subunits and retains some for the Board as a whole. Some decisions may have to be filtered through various committees; for example, if the public policy committee requires funds over and above its budget, it will need clear procedures for addressing the finance committee. If the campus ministry division requires a new staff person at one of the colleges, it may need either its own personnel committee or one in the Board, and *that* committee may need a liaison group of some sort with the bishop and cabinet.

The Board as a whole bears ultimate responsibility for its entire program. For the most part, that responsibility is fulfilled through two routine procedures:

• program and budget planning and approval
• program review and evaluation

Wherever program ideas originate, and wherever responsibility for carrying them out lies, all streams of responsibility eventually flow to the entire Board.

That doesn't mean that the entire Board must make every minute decision. The Board's procedures show how it has chosen to distribute the responsibility for making decisions. There are two fundamental questions that must be answered as a Board establishes it procedures:

a. What decisions must, in *all* cases, be made by the entire Board (excluding yearly planning and evaluation)?

b. What decisions may be, on a routine basis, made by task forces, standing committees, and divisions, and need only be reported to the Board?

In the light of those questions, decide for each of the program areas the procedures to be followed to deal with issues that arise in:

- personnel
- finance
- property
- policy
- program

One way to do that is to draw a circle around each of those words. In the circle, write the kinds of decisions a program committee should be able to make. Outside the circle, write the kinds of decisions that should be made by the Board as a whole or by an administrative committee of the Board.

An example might be dealing with property in campus ministry. Normally, the yearly budget of the Board would allot some money for routine repair and maintenance of campus ministry property. Decisions about the specific maintenance projects might well be made by the campus ministry committee together with the local campus ministry unit. But if major maintenance is required, or if new property is to be purchased, or if a decision about rental of property is to be made, the rule might be to take those decisions to the Board or one of its administrative committees.

The Board will have other procedures to settle on. For example, reporting from program areas to the whole, budget building, agenda planning, and appropriations.

2. Choosing Strategies.

The Board's plan for work in any of its program areas is its strategy. Strategies will be determined, to some extent, by the management tasks the *Discipline* assigns to the Board. They will also be affected by the number of institutions to which the Board relates and the extent of the programming the Board chooses to carry out. Several ingredients of strategy building are discussed in the chapters on campus ministry; schools, colleges, and universities; public policy; and the annual conference.

The primary aspect of strategy, however, should be considered here. That has to do with the Board's relationship to the institutions with which it works. Those may be ecumenical agencies, campus ministries, or schools, colleges, and universities. In each case, the Board has some degree of management authority and control. It must determine the degree of authority it has, and the degree to which it will be delegated.

The degrees of authority and control can be viewed in a spectrum.

Total Managerial Supervision				Negotiated Supervision			Delegated Supervision		
1	2	3	4	5	6	7	8	9	10

Total supervision means that, for example, the Board could set the institution's goals and policies.

Negotiated supervision presumes the final authority in some areas rests with the Board; but for reasons of law, charter, mission, or good management, it is shared with the institution. For example, the Board's actual authority over colleges is limited by reason both of law and charter. But the Board does have responsibility for the college's access to the conference. With a Wesley Foundation, matters lie differently. The Board has choices about the degree of autonomy offered to the Wesley Board in many of its functions: personnel, property, finances, and so on.

Delegated supervision grants the greatest degree of authority to the institution or agency related to the Board. That is, authority that is the Board's prerogative has been given to the other agencies. The Board retains the right to enter the program at significant times (the *Discipline* gives it that responsibility), but generally functions as a background and support system for the institutions and agencies.

The decision about supervision ought not be de facto. The Board is amenable to the annual conference for the programs of the conference. Its decisions about supervision and about different patterns of supervision vis-a-vis different agencies must reflect a clear rationale. Ultimately, no matter what style the Board uses for managing its strategy in any program area, it is responsible for that style and those programs.

Step Five: Assign Responsibilities

Committee assignments determine whether or not work gets done, and whether it gets done in a fair and considered way. When assigning responsibilities to committees:

a. **Keep a clear line between administrative (or support) functions and program committees.** Every Board member should serve on a program committee, guaranteeing that programs will be primary and that every program committee or task force will have a voice in administrative committees.

b. **Allow representatives of constituents a voice on the committee that programs for them.** Campus ministers should have access to the campus ministry committee; representatives of colleges and universities should have access to the schools, colleges, and universities committee. In no case should they be majority members, nor should campus ministers or college officers from church-related institutions necessarily be voting members of standing committees. Representatives from each group, present as consultants, will suffice for routine meetings. When budget or evaluation hearings are held, the Board may decide how many others to invite.

c. **Have representatives of districts on each standing committee.** That not only creates a good distribution from throughout the annual conference, it places knowledgeable representatives in each committee. An exception to this rule may occur if the Board creates a standing committee on the district and local church. In that case, the committee could have district representatives as its members.

d. **Distribute membership to each committee on the basis of workload.** In some conferences, the campus ministry committee may have several units to supervise, have an ecumenical convenant to evaluate and renegotiate yearly, have property to maintain, and have several on-site evaluations each year. That committee will need to be large and may have to be augmented by several persons working with it with voice but not vote.

It may also be the case that a new thrust in schools, colleges, and universities has been planned, one that involves massive fund-raising, vigorous student recruitment, and a conference-wide education program about the Black College Fund. Clearly, that program will require a large committee. On the other hand, during an inquiry and research stage of new programs, often small committees are better able to organize and get work done.

e. **Keep administrative and support committees small.** Because they must meet either before or after regular Board meetings, and often between them, those committees should be kept at minimal size for managing their work. Their tasks are to synthesize data, to plan agenda for Board meetings, to negotiate with the cabinet and with CCOM and CCFA on behalf of the Board. If they become large, they tend to extend their tasks into program, usually to the detriment of the Board and its work.

f. **Balance lay and clergy representation throughout the committees, making every effort to ensure the presence of ethnic minority persons and women.**

g. **Measure the personal interest and personal ability of members.** Most persons are interested in things they know about; their reluctance to serve in some areas results from lack of experience. Encourage persons to serve where their talents will best help the Board. A talent and interest questionnaire, filled out by each Board member and turned in prior to the Board's first meeting, will help the chair assess the array of talent available and suggest workable distributions of people.

h. **Make certain each committee has enough persons from the previous quadrennium to guarantee continuity in programming.**

Step Six: Evaluate

The Annual Conference Board should use three cycles of evaluation:

1. routine yearly reports from all program areas and institutions;
2. intense evaluation of one program area each year;
3. total evaluation of mission, organization, and program once every six years.

Evaluation should be a part of the working calendar of the Board and of every one of its committees. It should also be standard procedure for every agency that relates to the annual conference through the Board. The processes need not be onerous, but they must be pertinent and exact. They must also be clearly understood by all committees and agencies.

The details of evaluation used by any Board must be fashioned by the Board to meet its own needs. However, those who are to be evaluated should be consulted from the beginning, to be certain that evaluation tools properly reflect their work and retrieve information truly useful to them and to the Board. If there is one rule in selecting tools for effective evaluation, that rule is: CONSULT WITH THOSE YOU ARE EVALUATING AND DO SO FROM THE START.

For the purposes of keeping itself on track toward its goals, and of assessing those goals in the light of new needs, the Board should regularly take its pulse, frequently examine certain of its behaviors, and periodically have a complete physical. The following ideas will help.

Receive reports routinely.

Three kinds of reports ought to be received routinely by the Board from every committee and division and from every agency related to the Board:

- program and budget reports for the past year
- program and budget projections for the next year
- program and budget progress reports for the present year

Normally, prior to the beginning of each fiscal year, budget and program summaries (including descriptions of actual programs and evaluations of their effects) for the year immediately past should be presented. At the same time, budgets and program projections (again, including descriptions of programs, this time accompanied by goals for each) for the fiscal year beginning in one year should be presented for approval. (For example, if your fiscal year is the calendar year, before January, 1992, you would receive budget and program reports for 1991 and projections for 1993.)

During the year the Board should receive reports from each committee and agency containing current budget information and progress reports on programs. Those reports should also describe needed adjustments in the budget or program.

All reports should be on a standardized format so they can be completed with minimum difficulty and interpreted with maximum efficiency. It is not necessary that the Board's meetings be absorbed with the hearing of reports. Committees should receive progress reports and monitor them. Problems, of course, may become the business of the whole Board.

Annual reports and projects should receive the attention of the entire Board. They should come through appropriate committees and be ready for Board action. In each case, Board approval involves approval of the budget and the program goals.

Do an intensive evaluation of one program each year.

Once the Board has established its program and designed its structure, it should adopt a policy of evaluating one of its program areas intensively each year. To do intensive evaluations of all programs yearly monopolizes too much of the Board's limited time. To do no intensive evaluation leaves the Board ill equipped to explain and, if necessary, defend its work in the annual conference.

Intensive evaluation has other benefits. The program committees and agencies involved need to measure their effectiveness, not solely on a year-to-year basis, but over a longer stretch. Viewed over several years, trends and tendencies, cycles and anomalies become visible. Some programs that seem to have been in perpetual crisis may be seen, when examined over a three or four year period, to have made decisive gains. Others that have been applauded because of their ease of management may prove to have been easy, not because of their fine leadership but because of their triviality.

Intensive evaluation differs from routine reporting in several ways:

a. Intensive evaluation asks about the actual results of a program over several years.
b. Intensive evaluation asks, not only if the program met its goals, but whether the goals have proven worthwhile.
c. Intensive evaluation measures cost for program, personnel, and facilities over several years.
d. Intensive evaluation questions entire strategies and may result in midcourse corrections or comprehensive changes.
e. Intensive evaluation should involve external data (data in addition to routine reports) such as surveys of people affected by the programs, interviews with select members of the annual conference, and the use of professional or general church consultants.

As the result of intensive evaluation, the Board may decide to retain a program as it is, to make minor adjustments, to totally revise the program, or to end it altogether. It is especially important, when evaluating annual conference programs in campus ministry or with schools, colleges, and universities, that representatives of those agencies share in the design of the evaluation.

Do a total evaluation of the Board once every six years. Wherever possible, do it in conjunction with Board-wide planning.
Intensive evaluation asks about the effectiveness of specific programs over several years. Total evaluation asks about the effectiveness of the Board as a whole over several years.
Total Evaluation:

a. reviews the results of the work of each program area through summaries of their intensive evaluations;
b. isolates programs that have continued successfully, that have required adjustments, and that have failed, and determines reasons for those results;
c. asks if the Board's programs have achieved its goals;
d. asks if the Board's goals have fulfilled its mission;
e. asks if the Board's structure is adequate for its work;
f. asks if the annual conference has adequately understood and supported the work of the Board.

Total evaluation has two thrusts. The first is toward a comprehensive summation of the Board's performance over a six year span. The other is toward redesigning the Board for its next six years. Therefore, the summary could take the place of step one of the Six Step Planning Process.
To carry out the comprehensive summation, the Board should create a committee made up of representatives of the following groups:

• the Annual Conference Board of Higher Education and Campus Ministry
• the agencies the Board relates to, such as United Methodist schools, colleges, and

universities; Wesley Foundations; ecumenical campus ministries supported by the United Methodist Church

- the Board's program committees
- the cabinet
- the conference Council on Ministries
- the annual conference Council staff

The evaluation committee should be organized and monitored by the Annual Conference Board. The committee's report should be given to the Board, and all decisions about how to respond to the report should be made by the Board.

The report should clearly state the Board's mission, describe its performance, assess its structure and process, and suggest both minute and sweeping changes, as they seem appropriate.

Conclusion

The Six Step Planning Process should guide the Board toward well-stated programs and well-organized procedures. It should keep the distinction between programs and administration clean. And it should keep the Board in a steady process of self-scrutiny—resulting in a strong sense of direction and a useful degree of flexibility.

Chapter Ten

The Area Commission On Higher Education And Campus Ministry

Many annual conferences do much of their ministry in higher education through an Area Commission. In some, the Commission deals only with campus ministry. Separate entities exist to care for church-related colleges. Other Commissions combine responsibilities, managing programs with both colleges and campus ministries.

What are Area Commissions and why do some annual conferences have them? The word *area* refers to an episcopal area—the conferences served (or once served) by one bishop. Changes in conference boundaries and episcopal assignments have altered the situation in many places. Area Commissions now may be found where either or both of these conditions hold for two or more annual conferences:

1. Both conferences own or support the same schools, colleges, Wesley Foundations, or other campus ministries;
2. Both conferences do all of their campus ministry ecumenically, supporting ministries on the same campuses or through the same state ecumenical commission.

Commissions help avoid the complications that arise for institutions that relate to two annual conferences—duplications in evaluations and funding requests and confusion arising from dealing with different structures in each conference.

Commissions also help avoid complications for annual conferences by coordinating their efforts and by supplying a unified approach to working with institutions.

Area Commissions usually focus on campus ministry and church-related colleges. They have constitutions adopted by the participating annual conferences and often carry out a full range of managerial practices in policy, procedure, program, personnel, principal, property, and promotion.

Area Commissions and the Annual Conference Board

Area Commissions continue to be excellent options for ministry in higher education. But, since 1980, when the church created the Annual Conference Board and broadened the scope of ministry in higher education, there has arisen a need to examine them to find out:

- which of the new responsibilities the Commissions might assume;
- which responsibilities would best be carried out by the Annual Conference Board;
- how Area Commissions should be organized in order to satisfy the requirements of the *Discipline.*

The *Discipline* affirms the value of the Area Commission of Higher Education and Campus Ministry. It also lays out certain preconditions for forming or retaining them. Under the "General Responsibilities" of the Annual Conference Board of Higher Education and Campus Ministry it states:

> **To provide that two or more annual conferences may, on recommendation of their Boards of Higher Education and Campus Ministry, join in constituting an area or regional Committee or Commission on Higher Education and Campus Ministry, the membership, scope, and functions of which shall be determined by the cooperating conferences, in consultation with their bishop or bishops. The area committee or commission shall include a majority of its members from the participating Annual Conference Boards of Higher Education and Campus Ministry, with appropriate representation of college presidents, campus ministers, students and ethnic persons. [par. 732.4a(23)]**

Area Commissions, according to the *Discipline,* are to be formed:

- on the recommendation of Annual Conference Boards;
- in consultation with the bishop or bishops;
- by approval of the annual conference;
- with majority representation by members of the Annual Conference Boards;
- with appropriate representation of students and ethnic minority persons.

Clearly, the recommendation of the Annual Conference Board is the basis for inaugurating Commissions, or for continuing them. Those Boards, on behalf of the annual conference, must determine how much of the annual conference's ministry in higher education ought to be done through an Area Commission and how much must be done by the Board itself.

Because Annual Conference Boards did not exist when most Area Commissions were formed and because the work of ministry in higher education is more extensive now, Boards will have to make a fresh appraisal of the Commissions. They should work with the Commissions to prepare a proposal to take to the annual conferences—one that describes the full ministry in higher education and indicates which agency will assume which responsibilities. The proposal will have to indicate how the Area Commission relates to the Annual Conference Board. The Board manages the annual conference program in higher education, and it is the Board, therefore, that manages the annual conference's relationship to the Commission.

Considerations of how to distribute responsibilities between Boards and Commissions should provide satisfactory answers to these questions:

a. Which distribution of responsibilities will assure that all of the program areas are adequately accounted for (Public Policy, Campus Ministry, Schools and Colleges, Districts and local churches, and the annual conference)?
b. Which structure will guarantee an effective presence for higher education in each annual conference Council on Ministries and Council on Finance and Administration?
c. Which structure will best keep districts and local churches close to campus ministries and church-related colleges, and will allow for the most effective district and local church programs?

Some Patterns for Relating the Work of the Annual Conference to the Area Commission on Higher Education and Campus Ministry

The relationship of the Board to the Area Commission may take any of several forms. Each will have to assume the shape needed for its institutions and its ministries. Here are three possibilities:

Pattern One: A Self-Governing Commission.

The annual conferences consolidate their Boards of Higher Education and Campus Ministry into the Area Commission. The Commission assumes all responsibility for higher education programs, for team-building, and for relationships to the Council on Ministry and the Council on Finance and Administration of each annual conference. The Commission is a place of decision.

Pattern Two: A Liaison Commission.

The annual conferences retain total control of every phase of the higher education program. The Commission acts as liaison committee between the two Boards, suggesting plans and procedures that must be returned to each Board for ratification. The Commission is a place for negotiation between Boards.

Pattern Three: A Representative Commission.

The annual conferences determine specific areas of ministry that will be carried out by the Commission. The Commission is composed primarily of members of the Boards, who represent their Boards in the Commission and the Commission in their Board. Within the perimeter of agreement the Commission exercises a good deal of authority, but must account for its work to the Boards. The Commission is a place for delegated authority.

Each of the patterns has strengths and weaknesses. No matter which one is chosen, ingenuity will be required to make certain the total ministry in higher education is carried out. For example, Pattern One has the virtue of keeping a single, straight line of management between the Commission and the schools, colleges, and campus ministries. It has the greatest difficulty in maintaining systematic and effective contact with the conference Councils on Ministry and Finance and Administration, and with the districts and local churches.

Pattern Two has the virtue of keeping the ministry in higher education tightly integrated with the annual conference councils, districts, and local churches—after all, the same Board that works with them also figures prominently in every decision about campus ministry, public policy, and schools and colleges. But it creates a very slow process of decision-making, forcing all issues to be negotiated in the Commission and then reevaluated by each Board.

Pattern Three has the virtues of keeping a straight-line relationship between the Commission and the institutions and of allowing Boards to be involved and informed enough to represent higher education within the districts, local churches, and conference councils. But it makes the greatest demands on the elected members usually, requiring more persons to be active on both the Board and the Area Commission.

A Suggested Model for Working With an Area Commission on Higher Education and Campus Ministry

This model does not describe the only way for working with Area Commissions. It does describe briefly one way to distribute responsibilities that ensures attention to the entire program of ministry in higher education.

Tasks of the Commission.

The Area Commission assumes principal responsibility for managing the programs with campus ministries and church-related colleges. The Commission works within the policies agreed upon by the Annual Conference Boards, and all policies proposed by the Commission must be approved by both Boards. Other than that, the Commission has responsibility for all of the procedures, personnel, and property that would normally fall to the Annual Conference Board.

In funding, the Commission proposes budgets, including salaries, and recommends the appropriate contribution from each annual conference. It also receives and distributes the funds from each annual conference. However, it does not raise funds.

Tasks of the Boards.

The Boards assume full responsibility for public policy and for working with districts and local churches. They represent the total higher education program on the floor of annual conference and in the Councils on Ministries and Finance and Administration.

The Boards assume the responsibility for promoting the campus ministries and church-related colleges, using the entire connectional structure of the annual conference to do so. They also present the budgets for colleges and campus ministries and are responsible for raising their annual conference's portion of the Commission budget.

Membership on the Commission.

The vast majority of Commission members must be members of the Annual Conference Boards. They include representatives from districts in which campus ministries and church-related colleges are located and, where possible, a United Methodist trustee from each conference-related college. The district representatives are also ex officio members of the campus ministry boards within their Districts.

Organization of the Commission.

The commission is organized principally to accomplish its program. The chairs of the Annual Conference Boards serve on the Commission executive committee. Administrative committees are kept to a minimum and, where possible, administrative functions are incorporated into the program committees. Further, all committees have strong representation from each annual conference (for the purpose of knowledgeable, firsthand reporting).

The organization could include two Divisions: a Division of Schools and Colleges and a Division of Campus Ministry. Each Division is responsible for developing and monitoring the budget for its program, for appropriate evaluation procedures, for counseling with personnel, and for dealing with property concerns. An Executive Committee plans the Commission calendar for budgeting, reporting, and evaluation, and coordinates the Divisions. Both Divisions are responsible to the Commission for carrying out their programs.

Organization of the Boards.

Boards have program committees for Public Policy and for Connectional Relations (districts, local churches, annual conference, and conference councils). Both committees have substantial representation from members who also serve on the Commission. The Connectional Relations Committee also has all district representatives in its membership. The Board chair serves on the Conference Council on Ministries and represents higher education in other arenas in the annual conference.

The Board will need a Finance Committee, both to present its budget to the annual conference for apportionment to the churches and to raise additional funds to complete its commitments.

Measured by the questions raised at the end of the first section of this chapter, a structure like this:

- guarantees that all of the responsibilities for program areas are accounted for;
- guarantees an effective presence on the Conference Council on Ministries and, where needed, on the Council on Finance and Administration;
- guarantees close ties with districts and local churches.

This model may not be the one you choose. But it does illustrate one way to relate the Area Commission and the Annual Conference Board that takes account of all of the tasks assigned to the Board.

Conclusion

Area Commissions can augment the effectiveness of an Annual Conference Board. But to do so, their organization must allow the Commissions to do their work and yet retain a clear line of accountability between the Commission and the Annual Conference Board.

Commissions have no more power or effectiveness than the Annual Conference Boards allow them. They exist as instruments of the cooperating conferences. They will function best where careful thought has been given to:

- the full ministry in higher education;
- the simplest and most economical management of relationships with colleges and campus ministries;
- the most direct and powerful access to districts, local churches, and other annual conference agencies.

NOTES

NOTES

NOTES